D1484597

PRECISION

A Reference Handbook
for Writers

Robert J. Gula

UNIVERSITY
PRESS OF
AMERICA

LANHAM • NEW YORK • LONDON

Copyright © 1984 by

University Press of America,™ Inc.

4720 Boston Way
Lanham, MD 20706

3 Henrietta Street
London WC2E 8LU England

Copyright © 1980 by
Winthrop Publishers, Inc.

Library of Congress Cataloging in Publication Data

Gula, Robert J.
   Precision, a reference handbook for writers.

   Reprint. Originally published: Cambridge, Mass. :
Winthrop Publishers, c1980.
   Bibliography: p.
   Includes index.
   1. English language–Grammar–1950–   . 2.
English language–Punctuation. I. Title.
[PE1106.G84   1984]   428.2   83–21810
ISBN 0–8191–3688–3 (pbk. : alk. paper)

Contents

CONTENTS

Glossaries   201

Preface

Precision: A Reference Handbook for Writers is designed for anyone interested in precision: precision in thinking, in analyzing, in writing, and in communicating. It attempts to put between two covers as many areas of technical expertise as students of English may ever need to consult. Hence it includes sections on grammar and syntax, punctuation and mechanics, spelling, usage, documentation, sentence structure, paragraph unity and development, literary terms, and manuscript presentation. It is designed primarily as a reference book. The explanations are brief and the illustrations simple. Problems of writing have been itemized and isolated as discretely as possible under various headings; since some items apply to more than one heading, however, there is often duplication among the various chapters for the sake of thoroughness.

This book is not designed as a rhetoric; its aim is to serve as a resource to those who wish to use the language as accurately, precisely, and correctly as possible. It therefore by and large assumes a context of formal writing. Some of the entries may seem petty: does anyone care about the difference between *compare to* and *compare with,* for instance? Educated people should at least be aware that there is a distinction between the two. They can then honor or disregard that distinction at their discretion. But if they use *disinterested* instead of *uninterested,* they are exposing themselves to misinterpretation. It is such misinterpretation that this book has been designed to combat. If one knows the dangers, one can then avoid those dangers. Precision is not an end in itself, but it does help to make one less vulnerable and to assist one in communicating effectively.

A final word: the reader should realize that many of the rules cited throughout these pages are not absolute. There is no single standard, for instance, regarding the use of the comma, just as there is no invariable, universal standard regarding the principles of mechanics and usage. There are generally accepted conventions, but the rules for stylistic correctness are not graven in stone. Language is constantly changing, and the conventions change with the language. All one need do is read contemporary writing and one will see considerable variation in style; and certainly if one were to read even a paragraph from Dickens or Hawthorne, for instance, one would immediately see how much the principles of style have changed. We do need some generally accepted guidelines but, far more important, we should attempt to understand the reasons behind those guidelines. A mindless adherence to the rules can result in bad writing just as effectively as a complete ignorance of those rules. This is not to say that we are free to disregard the conventions at will, but it is to say that we should be willing to accept variations in style and that we should constantly be educating ourselves by noticing how writers, both good and bad, use the conventions. Our writing should be precise but at the same time it should be sensitive. The comma, for instance, is not an end in itself; it is a service to the reader. A dangling modifier is not intrinsically wrong; rather it leads to possible misinterpretation. And while one can still make one's point by using a plural verb after *neither,* doing so can distract the reader. It is such distraction and such misinterpretation that the "rules" help one to avoid, and it is the responsibility of the mature writer to use those rules but to do so with sensitivity and understanding, realizing that what may be appropriate in one context may not be appropriate in a different context.

language

1

On Speaking

The type of language that we use varies with the person with whom we are speaking and the context in which we are speaking. We use one level of language when we talk to a child, another when we talk to a peer, and still another when we talk to a superior. We use one type of language when we write a letter to a friend and a different type when we write a letter to a potential employer. Our language differs in moments of recreation and moments of business.

Many labels have been attached to the different types of diction: slang, colloquial, regional, archaic, obsolete, poetic, British. Then there are the broader categories, such as formal, informal, general, standard, nonstandard, substandard, illiterate.

This book will make only three distinctions: formal, informal, and substandard.

Formal English is what we use when we engage in scholarly pursuits; college writing; term, research, and technical papers; letters to potential employers; professional correspondence; and so on. Formal English acknowledges all the conventions of grammar, sentence structure, punctuation, mechanics, and word usage. Informal English is what we use in most of our communication—in our discussions and conversations. Informal English acknowledges most of the conventions of grammar, style, and usage, but it is, as its name suggests, more relaxed than formal English. We may also use substandard English from time to time. Substandard language incorporates slang and vulgarity, and it frequently ignores the conventions of grammar and usage.

It is important to be aware of the different types and levels of diction, not because there is anything intrinsically important about these levels, but because we should realize that what is appropriate in one context may not be appropriate in another. We should be in sufficient control of our language to be able to switch levels of diction when the occasion demands it.

The introductory chapter of this book is devoted to informal — particularly spoken — English. It is fine for speech to be informal. At the same time, the purpose of speech is to communicate, and effective communication depends upon some degree of precision. There are dangers in being too informal; this chapter will try to explain some of those dangers. Certain sloppy habits have entered our speech, often without our realizing it, and we would profit from breaking those habits. Therefore, let us make an effort to deprogram ourselves:

---

1 A   From the use of crutch words:

you know   like   I mean   right   really   sort of

The following account is not as close to parody as one might think:

I was sort of driving from Philadelphia to Pittsburgh, you know, and it was raining, I mean it was really raining, and like the roads were wet, and this guy — like he was really out of it — and he started to pass me, right! and like he lost control of the car, you know, and the next thing he was sort of over the guard rail. I mean, like I was scared!

One may defend the speaker of this passage by saying that this is merely a very colloquial form of discourse. Regardless, the speaker makes such a use of crutch words that many listeners will become distracted and put off. They may rightly or wrongly suspect that they are listening to an empty-headed person. Whether we like it or not, our speech often elicits a judgment from our audience, and if our speech is muddled, the judgment may be unfavorable.

---

1 B From an indiscriminate use of adjectives and adverbs:

basically	really	amazing	fantastic	incredible
obviously	nice	good	interesting	just

Basically all I really want is to graduate with honors.
His pitching was fantastic.
The movie was amazing.
I just know that the weekend will be fabulous.

Amazing, fantastic, incredible and other such powerful adjectives should be reserved for truly extreme reactions and should not be used as synonyms for *good* or *better than usual.* Similarly, *good* should not be used as a euphemism for *satisfactory.*

If we are indiscriminate in our use of strong adjectives and adverbs, what will we say when we truly want to express an extreme reaction? Like the boy who cried wolf, excessive use of hyperbole will make true hyperbole impossible.

The use of *just* illustrated above often indicates vapidity masquerading as wisdom and often bespeaks sham sincerity.

Nice and *interesting* are almost meaningless in contemporary speech; in fact, they may suggest that the speaker doesn't know how to react and is reluctant to express an opinion:

X: What do you think of my new painting?
Y: Oh, I think it's very interesting.

Most likely speaker Y either doesn't understand the painting or else doesn't like it. Otherwise, he would have responded with more depth — or at least more precision.

Obvious(ly) is often used dogmatically to camouflage an opinion or a generality:

Obviously President Carter was foolish for sponsoring and signing the Panama Canal treaty.

There is nothing obvious about this situation. It is a complex situation and deserves far more than a verbal curtsy. This statement parades as fact what is an opinion.

---

1 C   From an indiscriminate use of adverbs of degree:

very   quite   rather   somewhat   extremely

These poems are somewhat unique.

Either they're unique or they're not.

I was rather happy to see Sarah.

Is the speaker suggesting that he or she was only somewhat happy to see Sarah, not wholeheartedly happy?

When we use these adverbs indiscriminately, we run the risk of distorting our true meaning.

---

1 D   From using vague nouns and pronouns:

stuff   things   things like that
something   whatever

I like math and things like that.
He said that he was tired or something.
You can go to a game or watch TV or whatever.

The problem with such expressions is that they suggest that the speaker himself is unsure of what he is talking about.

---

1 E   From the indiscriminate use of the verb *love* and of verbs of *thinking:*

I love cashews.
I'd love to hear your opinions on this matter.
I'm sure that there's a gas station at the next exit.
I think that she should have come to the meeting.
I just know that he's the one who informed the boss.

Love describes an intense emotional experience, one hardly fitting for cashews, baseball games, or favorite record albums. The colloquial use of this word is indeed widespread, but it still bespeaks a lack of precision in describing one's feelings.

The verb *think* connotes a mental process. Too often it is used to express one's likes, dislikes, biases, prejudices, hopes, frustrations. When people use the expression *I think,* rarely have they actually done any thinking at all; usually they are merely reacting emotionally.

Perhaps it would be better to substitute the verb *suspect* or *feel* in situations like these. Unless we know for a fact that there is a gas station at the next exit or that he was in fact the one who informed the boss, we should not pretend to do so.

---

1 F   From creating words in *-ize:*

optimize   maximize   culturize   radicalize
enablize   alienize   prioritize   finalize
summerize (as opposed to winterize)

We constantly hear these words on radio and television, and they constantly sound offensive. Words such as these are often used by speakers who have not thought out precisely what they want to say and hence resort to formulaic patterns to avoid careful thought.

---

1 G   From the use of *fun* before a noun and from the use of *-wise* as a suffix:

He had a fun time at the party.

He's not very good speedwise, but he's an excellent batter.

The comments relating to example 1 F also apply here.

George Orwell once asked writers to ask of themselves: Have I said anything that is avoidably ugly?*

Words in *-ize* and *-wise* are avoidably ugly. Avoid them!

---

1 H   From the use of contemporary clichés:

He's really *into* folk dancing. He thinks *that's where it's at.* She's *with it.*

It took a while for us to be able to *communicate,* but I *guess that's what interpersonal relationships are all about.*

Again, Orwell's comments are particularly apt:

If you use readymade phrases, you not only don't have to hunt about for words; you also don't have to bother with the rhythms of your sentences. . . . By using stale metaphors, similes, and idioms, you save much mental effort, at the cost of leaving your meaning vague, not only for your reader but for yourself.

---

1 I   From verbal sloppiness:

a) *All's* for *all that:*

All's I can remember is that you were rude.

b) *A whole 'nother* for *another* or *completely different:*

There was a whole 'nother aspect to the situation.

c) Abuse of the exhortation *let's:*

Let's everyone pitch in to make this campaign a success.

---

*George Orwell, "Politics and the English Language," in *Shooting an Elephant and Other Essays* by George Orwell, copyright 1945, 1946, 1949. Reprinted by permission of Harcourt Brace Jovanovich, Inc.

What the speaker should have said is:

Let everyone pitch in . . . .

or

I hope everyone will pitch in . . . .

d) Beginning a sentence with *plus:*

The mayor has fought for tax reform. Plus, he has improved the quality of our schools.

e) The illogical use of the conjunction *so:*

You'll recognize Bright Toothpaste by the snappy red box. So buy Bright.

f) The use of *and* instead of a word expressing consequence or instead of a mark of punctuation:

The cast has worked hard to make this play a good one, and we hope that you will all come.

Robert Browning and Elizabeth Barrett were famous lovers, and I'm going to read you some of their poems.

What the speakers meant was:

Since the cast has worked hard to make this play a good one, we hope that you will all come.

or

The cast has worked hard to make this play a good one; therefore, we hope that you will all come.

Robert Browning and Elizabeth Barrett were famous lovers. I'm going to read you some of their poems.

Words have meanings, and it is a responsibility of the speaker to honor those meanings. If we can use words to suit our fancy, we run the risk of inviting chaos reminiscent of Alice's world in *Through the Looking Glass:*

"When *I* use a word," Humpty Dumpty said, in a rather scornful tone, "it means just what I choose it to mean — neither more nor less."

"The question is," said Alice, "whether you *can* make words mean so many different things."

"The question is," said Humpty Dumpty, "which is to be master — that's all."

1 J   From the use of psychological jargon:

   A little psychology is a dangerous thing; pop psychologists are dangerous, for they tend to ignore the complexities and richness of a person and instead put that person into oversimplified and often distorted categories. Unless we are trained psychologists, we should not pretend to be.

1 K   From speaking irresponsibly:

   We should avoid thinking aloud – unless we make it clear that we are thinking aloud – and responding spontaneously, off the cuff. We should think before we speak and assume responsibility for our words. We should select our words carefully and mean what we say.

   This injunction is not as dogmatic as it may appear. A hasty, thoughtless, or careless remark can have severe consequences. Remember, speaking without thinking is like shooting without aiming.

Further reading

The *National Lampoon* (September, 1976) has an article called "Bad Words." It is irreverent but perceptive. Get a copy if you can. The Orwell essay "Politics and the English Language" is worth reading at least once a week. The two Edwin Newman books, *Strictly Speaking* and *A Civil Tongue,* also deal with the abuses of language; both are entertaining and refreshingly dogmatic. Wilson Follett's *Modern American Usage* and Fowler's *Dictionary of Modern English Usage* both make important distinctions between the tasteful use and the vulgar abuse of language.

2

The Sentence

The sentence is a complete unit of thought. It may consist of just one word, of a few words, or of many words:

Stop!
The music stopped when the conductor left the stage.
When the conductor suddenly stopped the music and left the stage, the audience was perplexed, for no one had ever before witnessed such a bizarre spectacle.

Regardless of how long the sentence is, it must contain a subject and a verb. The subject tells who or what the sentence is about; the verb tells what the subject is doing or what is happening to the subject.

2 A   The **subject** is always a noun or a pronoun:

Robert E. Lee surrendered at Appomattox on April 9, 1865.
He was regarded as an outstanding military leader.
The *surrender* officially ended the Civil War.

There may be more than one subject:

Harmony, melody, and *rhythm* are the three essential components of music.

A simple subject is just the noun or pronoun. A complete subject includes the noun or pronoun together with words that complete its meaning:

SIMPLE SUBJECT: That *woman* is a distinguished novelist.
COMPLETE SUBJECT: *That woman* is a distinguished novelist.

SIMPLE SUBJECT: The *woman* with the dark glasses is a distinguished novelist.
COMPLETE SUBJECT: *The woman with the dark glasses* is a distinguished novelist.

SIMPLE SUBJECT: *Knowing* how to write well is a valuable skill.
COMPLETE SUBJECT: *Knowing how to write well* is a valuable skill.

The subject of the sentence is sometimes anticipated:

It is your duty to provide responsible leadership.

The true structure of this sentence is:

To provide responsible leadership is your duty.

Sometimes the subject is understood:

Stop!

This sentence actually means *You stop!*

---

2 B   The **verb** can denote what the subject is doing, what is happening to the subject, or the state of being of the subject.

Frustration often *causes* anxiety.

The verb tells what the subject *(frustration)* does: it causes.

His frustration *was caused* by financial problems.

The verb tells what is happening to the subject: it was caused.

Frustration *is* a leading cause of anxiety.

The verb tells the state of being of the subject: it is.

The elements of the verb are sometimes separated:

I *did* not *trust* his sincerity.
Are you *going to join* us tonight?

What *did* the message *say?*
She *has* consistently *been* one of our most loyal supporters.
Why *has* he *been spreading* rumors?

---

2 C A word or a group of words will often complete the meaning of a verb. Words that complete the meaning of a verb are called **complements.** The simple complement is a single word; the full complement is the complement and the words that go with it. In the following sentences the simple complement is underlined and the full complement is in italics.

Frustration often causes *anxiety.*
Frustration is *a leading cause of anxiety.*
She became *very angry.*
She became *upset and worried.*

The verb together with its complements, if there are any, is called the **predicate.** The predicate tells what is said of the subject.

---

2 D A **simple sentence** is a complete thought that has one subject-predicate combination:

Louise, Donna, and I were planning to attend the concert.

A **compound sentence** has two or more of these combinations; each of the subject-predicate units expresses a complete thought and is joined by a word called a **conjunction,** a word like *and, but, or, for, nor.*

I wanted to attend the concert, but I was unwilling to pay the price of a ticket.

There are two complete thoughts joined in this compound sentence:

I wanted to attend the concert.
I was unwilling to pay the price of a ticket.

There can be even more compound elements:

I wanted to attend the concert, but I was unwilling to pay the price of a ticket, for I was saving my money for a trip this summer, and that trip was more important to me than anything else.

This sentence has four compounded elements:

I wanted to attend the concert.
I was unwilling to pay the price of a ticket.
I was saving my money for a trip this summer.
That trip was more important to me than anything else.

A third type of sentence is the **complex sentence.** A complex sentence has one subject-predicate unit that expresses a complete thought and at least one subject-predicate combination that expresses an incomplete thought:

As soon as the Grateful Dead announced a concert, people rushed in droves for tickets.

Complete thought: people rushed in droves for tickets
Incomplete thought: as soon as the Grateful Dead announced a concert

When I heard who had been involved in the accident, I rushed to the hospital.

Complete thought: I rushed to the hospital
Incomplete thought: when I heard
Incomplete thought: who had been involved in the accident

The combination of a compound and a complex sentence forms a **compound-complex sentence:**

Whenever I see an accident, I become unusually cautious, and I instinctively drive much more carefully.

Complete thought: I become unusually cautious
Complete thought: I instinctively drive much more carefully.
Incomplete thought: whenever I see an accident

People who are insensitive to others and who infringe upon the rights of others are often shunned, for no one welcomes the company of someone who is inconsiderate.

Complete thought: people are often shunned

Incomplete thought: who are insensitive to others

Incomplete thought: who infringe upon the rights of others

Complete thought: no one welcomes the company of someone

Incomplete thought: who is insensitive

The complete thought—a subject-predicate unit that can stand alone as a sentence—is called an **independent clause.** The incomplete thought—the subject-predicate unit that cannot stand alone as a sentence—is called a **subordinate clause.**

---

2 E If a group of words has only a subject or only a verb or only a predicate, that group of words is a **fragment.** In order for a group of words to be considered a sentence, it must contain both a subject and a verb (or predicate) and express a complete thought.

FRAGMENT: the figures carved in stone

SENTENCE: The figures were carved in stone.
The figures carved in stone served a religious function.

FRAGMENT: to frighten away the evil spirits

SENTENCE: The natives carved figures in stones to frighten away the evil spirits.
The purpose of the stone figures was this: to frighten away the evil spirits.

FRAGMENT: who drive carelessly

SENTENCE: People who drive carelessly are menaces.

FRAGMENT: whenever a celebrity visits the hotel

SENTENCE: Whenever a celebrity visits the hotel, people rush to get autographs.

2 THE SENTENCE

FRAGMENT: the senator being a man whom we can trust

SENTENCE: The senator being a man whom we can trust, I have no reservations about contributing to his campaign.

FRAGMENT: a painter whose works I very much admire

SENTENCE: Vincent van Gogh, a painter whose works I very much admire, adopted a bold and unconventional style.

Van Gogh is a painter whose works I very much admire.

It is sometimes permissible to write fragments:

They say that war is a concomitant of civilization, that it will always be present, that it invariably has both good and bad effects. Perhaps! I prefer to regard it as a curse, however, and a dispensable one at that.

The fragment *Perhaps!* can be regarded as a pause for emphasis, or it can be regarded as being elliptical, inviting the reader to supply the missing words: *Perhaps what they say has some merit!* or *Perhaps they're right!*

Steinbeck uses fragments to create a vivid setting and a feeling of both tension and urgency:

The Western Land, nervous under the beginning change. The Western States, nervous as horses before a thunderstorm. The great owners, nervous, sensing a change, knowing nothing of the nature of the change. The great owners, striking at the immediate thing, the widening government, the growing labor unity; striking at new taxes, at plans; not knowing these things are results, not causes. Results, not causes; results, not causes. The causes lie deep and simple—the causes are a hunger in a stomach, multiplied a million times; a hunger in a single soul, hunger for joy and some security, multiplied a million times; muscles and mind aching to grow, to work, to create, multiplied a million times.*

While fragments may occasionally be appropriate in informal writing or in narrative or descriptive writing, they

*John Steinbeck, *The Grapes of Wrath* (New York: The Viking Press, Inc., 1939), pp. 163–64.

are rarely appropriate in formal writing. And an accidental, unintentional fragment is quite a serious error. A wise rule of thumb is this: never write a sentence fragment unless you can justify it with a good reason. If you have any doubts, express your thought in a complete sentence.

3

Agreement: Subject and Verb

---

3 A The subject of a sentence or clause determines whether the verb will be singular or plural.

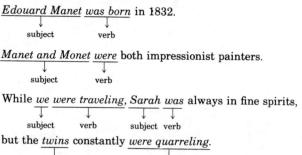

Edouard Manet was born in 1832.
subject   verb

Manet and Monet were both impressionist painters.
subject   verb

While *we were traveling, Sarah was* always in fine spirits,
subject   verb   subject verb

but the *twins* constantly *were quarreling*.
subject   verb

---

3 B A phrase that comes between the subject and its verb does not affect the verb.

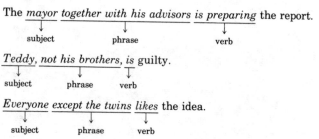

The *mayor together with his advisors is preparing* the report.
subject   phrase   verb

Teddy, not his brothers, is guilty.
subject   phrase   verb

Everyone except the twins likes the idea.
subject   phrase   verb

18

The *actors, not their director, are* responsible for the

    ↓   ↓   ↓

  subject   phrase   verb

success of this production.

---

3 C   Subjects joined by *and* take a plural verb.

Manet and Monet *are* often confused.

Both Hugh and David *were* abroad last summer.

---

3 D   When *there* anticipates a compound subject, the verb is singular if the first subject is singular, and plural if the first subject is plural.

There *is* a desk and two lamps in each room.

There *are* two lamps and a desk in each room.

---

3 E   The verb is not affected when the position of the subject is changed.

Where *were* Ted and Mary?

Is there a desk and a lamp in each room?

Are there desks and lamps in the rooms?

---

3 F   Sometimes *and* joins words that are thought of as one unit. In such a situation the verb is singular.

The owner and manager, Mr. Little, *is* planning to expand the business.

In this sentence Mr. Little is both owner and manager.

Bread and water *has* traditionally been considered the standard meal in prisons.

Bread and water is thought of as one item.

3 AGREEMENT: SUBJECT AND VERB

3 G   When subjects are joined by *or, either . . . or, nor, neither . . . nor*, the verb agrees with the nearer subject.

Neither Tyrone nor the twins *were* at the party.

Neither the twins nor Tyrone *was* at the party.

Either you or I *am* going to be editor of the yearbook.

3 H   It should be noted that informal discourse allows a plural verb after *or* and *nor*.

Neither the twins nor Tyrone were at the party.

Either you or I are going to be editor of the yearbook.

3 I   Indefinite pronouns—such as *each, everyone, any, anyone, somebody, someone, either, neither*—are singular and therefore take singular verbs.

Neither of the candidates *seems* qualified.

Is either of the candidates qualified for the position?

I had two choices; each *was* appealing.

If you note that *each* means *each one*, *neither* means *neither one*, *either* means *either one*, the reason for the singular verb becomes clear. The *of* phrase is merely an intervening one; hence, according to 3 B, it does not affect the verb.

3 J   When a prepositional phrase beginning with *of* follows fractions and words denoting a part or a portion—such as *some, the rest, all, none, part, a lot, most*—the object of the preposition determines whether the verb will be singular or plural.

20

Some of the document *has* been destroyed.

Some of the documents *have* been destroyed.

None of the message *was* intelligible.

None of the messages *were* intelligible.

A quarter of the project *is* completed.

A quarter of the students *are* studying history.

---

3 K   Expressions of amount — such as words of time, distance, weight, money, and measure — are singular when the amount is regarded as a whole. These expressions are plural when the units of the amount are regarded separately.

Ten dollars *is* too expensive for a necktie.

Five miles *is* not very far to walk.

but

The last five miles *were* the longest ones of our trip.

---

3 L   Arithmetical phrases are usually regarded as singular.

Six times five *is* thirty.

Seven minus two *is* five.

---

3 M   A collective noun — a noun that refers to a group, such as *team, crew, committee, class* — is singular when all the members of the group are being referred to together. The collective noun is plural when the sentence is stressing the different activities of the members of the group.

The committee *is* meeting now.

The committee *are* in complete disagreement.

In the second example, *committee* actually means *the separate members of the committee.*

3 N   Some plural nouns are thought of as a single unit and hence take a singular verb.

Mumps *is* no longer the dreaded disease that it once was.
The news tonight *is* distressing.

This principle is true for most nouns in *-ics*.

Economics *is* a difficult subject.

3 O   The expression *one of these/those . . . who/that . . .* will always be followed by a plural verb. But if the word *only* qualifies the expression, then the verb will be singular.

Hercules is one of those mythological figures that *keep* on appearing in literature.

Kathy is the only one of the students who *is* eligible for the award.

4

Pronouns: Agreement, Selection, Position

A pronoun is a word used in place of a noun. There are eight types:

a) The **personal pronoun**

1st person, singular: *I, mine, me*
1st person, plural: *we, ours, us*
2nd person, singular and plural: *you, yours*
3rd person, singular, masculine: *he, his, him*
3rd person, singular, feminine: *she, hers, her*
3rd person, singular, neuter: *it, its*
3rd person, plural: *they, theirs, them*

b) The **intensive pronoun**

I *myself*, we *ourselves*, you *yourself*, she *herself*, they *themselves*

c) The **reflexive pronoun**

I hurt *myself*, you hurt *yourself*, they hurt *themselves*, she hurt *herself*

d) The **relative pronoun**

who, whom, whose, which, that, whoever, whomever, whatever

The relative pronoun connects two clauses.

e) The **interrogative pronoun**

Who, Whose, Whom, What

The interrogative pronoun asks a question.

f) The demonstrative pronoun

this, that, these, those

g) The indefinite pronoun

someone, somebody, anyone, anybody, each, either, no one, nobody, neither

h) The reciprocal pronoun

they helped *each other*

The **antecedent** of a pronoun is the word or words that the pronoun stands for. In the sentences that follow, the pronoun is in italics and its antecedent is in boldface type.

Mozart composed several fine works while *he* still was a child.

I like this **wine**; I have no hesitation in recommending *it* to you.

Mr. Trollope forced *himself* to write each morning before *he* went to work.

The **song** *that* Joan wrote is beautiful.

People *who* live in glass houses shouldn't throw stones.

Michelangelo and **Leonardo da Vinci** are regarded as two of the most important painters of the Renaissance. *They* have never been equaled, although many people have tried to imitate *them.*

AGREEMENT OF PRONOUN AND ANTECEDENT

4 A If an antecedent is singular, then its pronoun must also be singular.

The committee is in *its* tenth hour of deliberation.

Each of the actors has *her* own particular style. (Section 3 I)

Neither Judy nor Liz has finished *her* project. (Section 3 G)

Everyone must do *her* share if this trip is going to be successful.

Either the *Times* or the *Tribune* has incorrectly presented *its* account of the accident. (Section 3 G)

The mayor together with his associates is ready to announce *his* plan. (Section 3 B)

Each of the witnesses had *his* own separate account of the accident. (Section 3 I)

---

4 B **If an antecedent is plural, then its pronoun must also be plural.**

Some of the students have already handed in *their* reports.

Since Matthew and Lucius were the first to volunteer *their* services, I have put *them* in charge of the project.

Both the *Times* and the *Tribune* have incorrectly presented *their* accounts of the accident.

Some of the witnesses seem to have changed *their* accounts of the accident.

---

4 C **Sometimes a strict adherence to the rules of agreement becomes unnatural.**

When everyone had finishing discussing the matter, the chairman asked him to vote.

In such a case, there may be a temptation to be informal:

When everyone had finished discussing the matter, the chairman asked them to vote.

But the problem can easily be avoided:

When everyone had finished discussing the matter, the chairman called for a vote.

or

When everyone had finished discussing the matter, the chairman asked the members (the committee) to vote.

---

4 D **Often one hears a statement such as**

Everyone enjoyed themselves at the party.

or

If anyone has lost their script, they can pick up another one at this afternoon's rehearsal.

Such expressions, although they are grammatically inaccurate (Section 3 I), are often an attempt to avoid the masculine bias implied by the singular masculine pronoun:

Everyone enjoyed *himself* at the party.

If **anyone** has lost *his* script, *he* can pick up another one at this afternoon's rehearsal.

Many speakers avoid this bias by expanding the pronoun:

Everyone enjoyed *himself and herself* at the party.

If **anyone** has lost *his or her* script, *he or she* can pick up another one at this afternoon's rehearsal.

Such expressions, however, while grammatically accurate, can be awkward, especially when the dual reference must be repeated several times in a sentence or paragraph. The problem can usually be avoided by simply not using an indefinite pronoun but rather by supplying a plural noun as an antecedent:

All the people at the party enjoyed *themselves.*

If any **members of the cast** have lost *their* scripts, *they* can pick up another copy at this afternoon's rehearsal.

If such a substitution is inappropriate, speakers must simply use their taste and judgment in selecting among the alternatives: incorrect grammar, masculine bias, or stilted phraseology.

---

4 E   Use *this/that* with singular nouns and *these/those* with plural nouns.

This is the kind (sort, type) of game that I enjoy.
These are the types (sorts, kinds) of games that I enjoy.

Make sure that the pronoun, the noun, and the object of *of* are either all singular or all plural.

SELECTION AND POSITION OF PRONOUNS

4 F   Pronouns should be used consistently. For instance, if the antecedent is in the third person, the pronoun must also be in the third person. The following example illustrates an inconsistent use of pronouns:

When an actor takes on a new assignment, *he* must be patient. *You* can't expect to know what *your* director wants during the first rehearsal. *One* must be willing to ask questions and to learn from *your* mistakes.

The antecedent in this passage is *an actor*. Therefore, a third-person pronoun is needed. Note how this passage shifts its pronouns from *he* to *you* to *one*. The passage should be rewritten using one pronoun consistently. Here are two ways of improving this passage:

Consistent second-person pronouns:

When *you* take on a new acting assignment, *you* must be patient. *You* can't expect to know what *your* director wants during the first rehearsal. *You* must be willing to ask questions and to learn from *your* mistakes.

Consistent third-person pronouns:

When an actor takes on a new assignment, *he* must be patient. *He* can't expect to know what *his* director wants during the first rehearsal. *He* must be willing to ask questions and to learn from *his* mistakes.

4 G   The impersonal pronoun *(one)* often sounds clumsy and unnatural, especially when it is used in a series. To make a sentence sound smoother, it is permissible to violate consistency and to substitute the personal pronoun *(he, him, his, himself)*.

Correct but stilted:

One must control *one's* anger lest *one* find *oneself* in unnecessary quarrels.

Correct but more natural:

One must control *his* anger lest *he* find *himself* in unnecessary quarrels.

or

A person must control *his* anger lest *he* find *himself* in unnecessary quarrels.

or

You must control *your* anger lest *you* find *yourself* in unnecessary quarrels.

---

4 H Note that *them* is a personal pronoun, not a demonstrative pronoun. Therefore, a sentence such as

Them kids are making a ruckus again.

should be expressed:

Those/These kids are making a ruckus again.

---

4 I The reflexive pronoun is not an elegant way to refer to yourself.

Don't say:

Jacques and *myself* have been chosen to attend the conference.
Jennifer told Darryl and *myself* about the party.

Instead, be natural and use the personal pronoun:

Jacques and *I* have been chosen to attend the conference.
Jennifer told Darryl and *me* about the party.

---

4 J Avoid putting the antecedent of a pronoun inside a subordinate clause. The reader can easily get confused, as in the following example:

The general, whose *hands* had been locked together behind his back, unclenched *them* and calmly smoothed his lapels.

Instead, put the antecedent in the main clause:

The general unclenched his *hands,* which had been locked together behind his back, and calmly smoothed his lapels.

---

4 K   A subtle distinction exists between the relative pronouns *which* and *that*. *Which* is usually used to introduce a clause *not essential* to the meaning of the sentence. *That* is always used to introduce a clause *essential* to the meaning of the sentence.

Cars, which have become a necessity to most people, are oftentimes a nuisance.

In this sentence, the words *which have become a necessity to most people* are not essential. They could have been omitted without distorting the meaning of the sentence.

Cars that are constantly breaking down should not be allowed on the road.

In this sentence, however, the words *that are constantly breaking down* are absolutely essential. If they were omitted, the meaning of the sentence would indeed be distorted: "Cars should not be allowed on the road."

Occasionally *which* will be used to introduce an essential clause, but only when the use of *that* would be awkward:

Do you realize that that letter (that/which) you just threw away contained the directions to our conference?

While the *that* is required grammatically, it would be the third use of the word in the sentence; to avoid such dissonance, *which* would be acceptable. Note that regardless of whether *that* or *which* introduces the essential clause, there is no comma before the relative pronoun. When the clause is not essential, however, there is always a comma before the pronoun.

4 L   Avoid using a possessive pronoun when an essential clause follows.

CLUMSY: Bernard lost *his* gloves that he had received as a gift from his aunt.

IMPROVED: Bernard lost *the* gloves that he had received as a gift from his aunt.

---

4 M   Do not begin a declarative sentence with a relative pronoun *(who, whose, whom, which, that).* Change the relative pronoun to a personal or to a demonstrative pronoun.

INCORRECT: I understand that the fire was deliberately set. Which is what I suspected all along.

CORRECT: I understand that the fire was deliberately set. *This* is what I suspected all along.

INCORRECT: I just saw a new play. Which is called *Under Stars.*

CORRECT: I just saw a new play. *It* is called *Under Stars.*

INCORRECT: I just met the mayor's assistant. Whose name is Wrampelmeier.

CORRECT: I just met the mayor's assistant. *His* name is Wrampelmeier.

5

Pronouns: Reference

When we talk about the *reference* of a pronoun, we are talking about the relationship between the pronoun and the word(s) to which the pronoun refers. Our goal is to make that relationship as clear and as precise as possible. If that relationship is not clear, we may confuse or mislead the reader.

5 A   Avoid vague or sloppy references. A pronoun should refer to one specific antecedent, not to a phrase or a clause or an idea.

Vague reference:

France and Britain gained many colonies during the late nineteenth century, *which* greatly upset Germany.

In this sentence, the pronoun *which* is being asked to refer to the whole introductory clause. Such a reference is inexact. The pronoun should refer to specific words only, not to a cluster of words. The reference can easily be improved:

France and Britain gained many colonies during the late nineteenth century; *these acquisitions* greatly upset Germany.

or

Germany was greatly upset when, during the late nineteenth century, France and Britain gained many colonies.

5

Note the abuse of the pronoun *this* in the following sentence:

There were three cases of arson within the past three weeks; *this* made the people in the neighborhood very apprehensive.

In this example, the pronoun *this* is trying to refer to a whole sentence. Again, such a reference is vague: were the people upset because of the three cases of arson, because the cases occurred within a three-week period, or because of both factors? The sentence can easily be rewritten to avoid the vagueness:

The three cases of arson within the past three weeks made the people in the neighborhood very apprehensive.

or

Since there were three cases of arson within three weeks, the people in the neighborhood were very apprehensive.

Avoid beginning a sentence with *this, that, these,* or *those* unless you use the word as an adjective: *this X, that X, these X's, those X's.*

---

5 B   Avoid ambiguous references. The antecedent of a pronoun should be clear. When a pronoun can refer to more than one antecedent, then the reference of that pronoun is ambiguous.

Nancy showed Louise the ring that *she* had wanted for such a long time.

In this sentence, the *she* could refer to either Nancy or Louise. The ambiguity can be removed by repeating the antecedent:

Nancy showed Louise the ring that *Louise* had wanted for such a long time.

Ambiguous:

Agamemnon and Achilles were two of the most important Greek warriors in the Trojan War; however, after Agamemnon appropriated Achilles' mistress Briseis, *he* withdrew from combat and refused to fight.

The *he* could refer to Agamemnon as well as to Achilles. The following revision removes the ambiguity:

Agamemnon and Achilles were two of the most important Greek warriors in the Trojan War. Achilles, however, after his mistress Briseis had been appropriated by Agamemnon, withdrew from combat and refused to fight.

---

5 C   Implied references should be made explicit. The pronoun should refer literally to the antecedent, not to some word implied by the antecedent or related to the antecedent.

I have always been interested in being a musician, but I don't think I'll major in *it* in college.

Here the *it* improperly refers to *musician* or *being a musician.* What the speaker means to say is

I have always been interested in being a musician, but I don't think I'll major in *music* in college.

or

I have always been interested in *music,* but I don't think I'll major in it in college.

A second example shows the same imprecision:

I have written a lot of poetry, but I can't get any of *them* published.

What the speaker actually means is

I have written a lot of poetry, but I can't get any of *my poems* published.

or

I have written a lot of *poems,* but I can't get any of them published.

A third example:

He speaks clearly and forcefully, and *this* makes him most effective.

What this speaker means is

He speaks clearly and forcefully and *these qualities* make him most effective.

or

His clear and forceful speech makes him most effective.

A fourth example:

Since *a snake* will rarely attack unless either surprised or provoked, their reputation as aggressors is an unfair one.

What this speaker might have said is:

Since *snakes* will rarely attack unless either surprised or provoked, *their* reputation as aggressors is an unfair one.

A fifth example:

She has just bought a new red car; it is her favorite color.

This sentence is saying that a car is a color. The imprecise reference can be easily corrected:

She has just bought a new red car; red is her favorite color.

In each of the five cases just cited, the pronoun is not referring accurately to its antecedent. The writer in each case is assigning the pronoun an antecedent that was not stated but rather that was implied or suggested.

---

5 D   Redundant pronouns should be eliminated. Do not use a pronoun as the subject of a verb if that verb already has an expressed subject, as the writer of the following sentence has incorrectly done:

The *commander,* after he had conducted several unsuccessful campaigns and had led his men to near defeat, realizing that his powers were declining, *he* decided to retire.

Even though the subject *(commander)* is considerably separated from its verb *(decided),* there is no need for the pronoun *he.* What the incorrect sentence actually says is *The commander . . . he decided to retire.*

---

5 E   Be careful not to confuse personal and impersonal pronouns. The personal pronouns *it* and *they* are often inappropriately used as if they were impersonal:

In Chapter 15 *it* lists the reasons for the war.

In the *Tribune they* are always making critical comments about the administration.

The pronoun *it* in the first sentence and the pronoun *they* in the second sentence have no antecedents. The sentences should be recast by removing the pronouns:

Chapter 15 lists the reasons for the war.

The *Tribune* is always making critical comments about the administration.

or

In the *Tribune* the writers (editors, editorials) are always making critical comments about the administration.

6

Pronouns: Case

Personal, relative, and interrogative pronouns change their spelling as they appear in different grammatical relationships within a sentence. These various relationships are expressed by *cases*. English has three cases: the *subject* (or *nominative*) case, the *possessive* case, and the *objective* case. The various spellings of pronouns in the different cases are as follows:

NOMINATIVE, OR SUBJECT CASE: *I, we, you, he, she, it, they, who*
POSSESSIVE CASE: *mine, ours, yours, his, hers, its, theirs, whose*
OBJECTIVE CASE: *me, us, you, him, her, it, them, whom*

---

6 A   Note that the possessive case of these pronouns does not use an apostrophe.

---

6 B   The nominative, or subject case is required for a pronoun that serves as the subject of a verb.

He and *I* will attend the convention.
Mary and *we* will travel together this summer.
It is clear that *you* and *they* are wrong.

---

6 C   The nominative case is also required when a pronoun serves as a predicate nominative—that is, when the pronoun is the same as the subject.

It is *I*.

So it was *he* that was guilty!

The guilty parties were Tim and *she*.

It surely must have been *they*.

This rule is obeyed in formal writing. It is frequently ignored in informal writing and speaking. Informal discourse finds *It's me* or *It was him* much more natural.

---

6 D   The objective case is required for a pronoun that is used as an object: as the direct object of a verb, as an indirect object, and as the object of a preposition. (See also Chapter 40, *case*.)

I showed *him* the puppies.   (*Him* is indirect object of the verb *showed*.)

I showed the puppies to *him*.   (*Him* is object of the preposition *to*.)

I will show *them* to you.   (*Them* is the direct object of the verb *show*.)

---

6 E   An attempt at politeness or overcorrectness often obscures the correct use of the proper case. In the following sentence:

Your sister gave the message to Peter and *I*.

the speaker is referring to himself last, as the conventions of politeness encourage him to do. But he is ignoring the fact that the construction of the sentence requires him to put himself in the objective case, since the pronoun is the object of the preposition *to*. He should have said

Your sister gave the message to Peter and *me*.

Another example:

I told him my suspicions, but I insisted that my remarks must be kept just between *he* and *I*.

Since *between* is a preposition, it requires the pronouns to be in the objective case:

I told him my suspicions, but I insisted that my remarks must be kept just between *him* and *me.*

---

6 F When pronouns qualify or rename a noun, they should be in the same case as that noun.

Only two people, *he* and *I,* will attend the conference.

Since *people* is the subject of the verb *will attend,* the qualifying pronouns should also be in the subject (nominative) case.

The letter was addressed to the four of us: Steven, Matthew, Peter, and *me.*

The letter was addressed to Steven, to Matthew, to Peter, and to me.

We politicians are always getting into trouble.   (Subject)

It is *we* politicians that will lead this city to greatness.   (Predicate nominative)

I hope that the people will give *us* politicians a vote of confidence.   (Indirect object)

The leadership of this city is in the hands of *us* politicians. (Object of a preposition)

The people trust *us* politicians.   (Direct object)

---

6 G When a pronoun is used as part of a comparison, the pronoun should have the same grammatical relationship to the sentence as the word it is being compared to.

I trust him more than $\begin{cases} \text{she.} \\ \text{her.} \end{cases}$

If *she* is used, the sentence means *I trust him more than she trusts him.* Since *she* is in the subject case, the word is being compared to the other subject of the sentence: *I.* On the other hand, if *her* is used, the sentence means *I trust him more than I trust her.* Here the two objects that are being compared are *him* and *her.*

---

6 H An infinitive — that is, a verb introduced by *to* — does not affect the case of a pronoun.

I suspect *them* to be guilty.

Them is the direct object of the verb *suspect.*

I suspect the guilty ones to be *them.*

Them is a complement of the direct object *guilty ones* and hence is in the objective case.

The guilty ones were thought to be *they.*

They is the complement of the subject of the sentence, *guilty ones;* hence, it is in the nominative case. This construction can easily be clarified by slightly recasting the sentence:

They were thought to be the guilty ones.

---

6 I A gerund is a verb form ending in *-ing* that is used as a noun — that is, as a subject or an object or any of the various ways that nouns are used. The possessive case of a pronoun is usually used before a gerund. In the following sentences, the possessive pronoun is in italics and the gerund in boldface.

I resent *your* **trying** to sneak out.

Her **entering** the contest took quite a bit of courage.

My **getting caught** was a source of embarrassment to the whole family.

Your **having rushed** him to the hospital saved his life.

7

Pronouns: Who, Whom

7 A   Even though the precise distinction between *who* and *whom* is becoming more and more restricted to formal discourse and even though it is largely ignored in our day-to-day speech, that distinction is not a difficult one. *Who* is used as the subject of a verb; *whom* is used as an object.

Marie Antoinette, who was guillotined in 1793, was perhaps guilty more of naïveté than of irresponsibility.

Who is the subject of *was guillotined.* The relationship is even clearer when the thoughts are separated:

Marie Antoinette was perhaps guilty more of naïveté than of irresponsibility. *She* was guillotined in 1793.

In the following sentence:

Marie Antoinette, whom the revolutionaries guillotined in 1793, was perhaps guilty more of naïveté than of irresponsibility.

Whom is the direct object of the verb *guillotined.* Again, dividing the sentence into its separate parts clarifies the relationship:

Marie Antoinette was perhaps guilty more of naïveté than of irresponsibility. The revolutionaries guillotined *her* in 1793.

7 B   Intervening expressions—such as *I feel, I believe, we know, they say, he thinks*—do not affect the case of the pronoun. (See Section 3 B.)

The mayor, who $\left\{\begin{array}{l} \text{I hear} \\ \text{we hope} \\ \text{the papers say} \end{array}\right\}$ is planning to retire, is incompetent.

Who is still the subject of the verb *is planning,* in spite of any intervening phrase.

---

7 C   The position of the pronoun does not affect the case. Regardless of the position of the pronoun, its case is determined by its grammatical function in the sentence.

Whom did the senator accuse of embezzling public funds?

Whom is the object of the verb *did . . . accuse.*

Whom are you talking about?

Whom is the object of the preposition *about.*

---

7 D   Observe the following sentence:

Everyone had suspicions about (who/whom) was guilty.

A writer may wonder whether the pronoun should take its case from the preposition *about* or from its function as the subject of the verb *was.* In sentences such as this one, the preposition has no effect upon the pronoun. The case of the pronoun should reflect its relationship to the words that it introduces. Hence, in the above illustration, the correct pronoun is *who,* since *who* is the subject of the verb.

I will give the reward to (whoever/whomever) I feel is most qualified.

The pronoun is the subject of the verb *is;* hence, the proper form is *whoever.* The words *I feel,* according to the rule for intervening expressions (3 B), have no effect upon the case of the pronoun.

But in the following sentence:

I will give the reward to whomever you recommend.

the pronoun is the direct object of the verb *recommend* and hence should be in the objective case: *whomever.*

---

7 E   When people are not sure which pronoun to select, *who* or *whom,* they will often choose *whom,* thinking that it is more learned or perhaps more elegant, and they will often come up with sentences that are badly strained. If faced with such a choice, select *who.* Even if you're wrong, at least you will sound natural. Ignorance masquerading behind casualness is better than ignorance masquerading behind pretentiousness.

8

Adjectives and Adverbs

An adjective is a word that describes or modifies a noun or pronoun; it usually answers the question *What kind of?* or *Which?*

The loud noise distracted me.

Loud describes *noise* and is therefore an adjective. It tells what kind of noise disturbed me.

Groups of words – phrases and clauses – can serve as adjectives. For instance in the sentence

A government *that serves only itself* will inevitably fall.

the italicized words specify what kind of government will inevitably fall; therefore, that group of words is a clause being used as an adjective to modify *government.*

Peter the Great was the first Russian ruler to realize the importance of technology.

The words *of technology* specify what kind of importance; therefore, this prepositional phrase is used as an adjective to modify *importance.*

An adverb is a word that qualifies or modifies a verb or an adjective or another adverb; it usually answers the question *How?* or *When?* or *Where?* or *Why?* or *To what extent?*

After Napoleon fought in Russia, his forces became so weakened that they could scarcely continue.

So is an adverb because it tells to what extent Napoleon's forces became weakened; it modifies the adjective *weakened. Scarcely* is also an adverb since it qualifies the verb *continue;* it tells to what extent Napoleon's forces could continue.

Groups of words – phrases and clauses – can serve as adverbs. In the above sentence, the words *after Napoleon fought in Russia* specify when Napoleon's forces became weakened; hence, this clause is used adverbially to modify the verb *became*. The phrase *in Russia* tells where Napoleon was fighting; hence, it serves as an adverb to modify the verb *fought*.

---

8 A   Verbs of the senses – such as *feel, taste, smell, sound* – often cause problems for a speaker trying to select a modifier. An adjective should complement these verbs when the speaker is describing his reaction.

The salad tastes *good*.   [not *well*]
Your voice sounds *clear*.   [not *clearly*]
I felt *confident*.   [not *confidently*]
The stew smells *bad*.   [not *badly*]

---

8 B   The above verbs of senses change their meaning when they are complemented by an adverb instead of an adjective.

ADJECTIVE: I felt confident. (I was confident. I had a sense of confidence.)

ADVERB: I felt the dog confidently. (I was using my sense of touch.)

If one were to say *The stew smells badly*, one would create the ludicrous image of the stew's smelling something – that is, using its sense of smell – and not doing a very good job at it.

---

8 C   Verbs such as *seem, appear, look, become*, and *grow* are usually equivalent to the verb *be* and therefore require an adjective to complete the sense.

The cake looks *good* to me.   [not *well*]
He appeared *sad*.   [not *sadly*]
I became *happy*.   [not *happily*]
She seemed *gracious*.   [not *graciously*]

---

8 D   An adverbial modifier with these verbs changes the meaning of the verb.

ADJECTIVE: The troops looked *despondent* to me.

Looked is equivalent to *seemed, appeared,* or *were*.

ADVERB: The troops looked *despondently* at the devastation.

Here the troops are actually using their sense of vision.

ADJECTIVE: The people grew *wild* when they heard the news.

Grew is equivalent to *became* or *were*.

ADVERB: The weeds grew *wildly* after the rain.

Here the weeds are actually growing.

---

8 E   *Well* is usually an adverb. However, it is also used as an adjective to refer to *good health*.

ADVERB: You played unusually well last night.
ADJECTIVE: I feel unusually well today.

Note: Expressions such as *Things are well* are actually elliptical—that is, a word or words have been omitted. The expression actually means *Things are going well;* hence, *well* is actually an adverb modifying the implied verb *going*.

---

8 F   It is important that adverbs be positioned precisely and unambiguously so as not to confuse the reader. In the following sentence:

His speaking seriously upset the Parliament.

one cannot tell whether he was speaking seriously or whether the Parliament was seriously upset. The sentence should be recast to remove the ambiguity:

The Parliament became seriously upset when he spoke.

or

The Parliament became upset when he spoke seriously.

Modifiers that are positioned ambiguously are sometimes called **squinting modifiers.** (See also Section 10 B.)

I nearly ran five miles yesterday.

If the point of the sentence is to stress the type of motion—I moved fairly fast but not fast enough to be called running—then the sentence is fine. But if the point of the sentence is to stress the distance, then the modifier is imprecisely positioned, and the speaker should have said:

I ran nearly five miles yesterday.

---

8 G *Real, good, sure,* and *some* are adjectives. They should not be used as adverbs.

INCORRECT: You are real clever.
We sure want to succeed.

CORRECT: You are really clever.
We surely want to succeed.

---

8 H Expressions like *is when, is because,* and *is where* are often incorrectly used. *When,* for instance, indicates time; it should not be used to introduce an explanation. Instead of saying *is when,* say *occurs when* or use a noun to complete the meaning.

INCORRECT: Photosynthesis is when carbon dioxide and water are converted into oxygen.

CORRECT: Photosynthesis occurs when carbon dioxide and water are converted into oxygen.

or

> Photosynthesis is the process by which carbon dioxide and water are converted into oxygen.

Instead of saying *is because,* say *is that* or simply supply a noun to complete the meaning:

INCORRECT: The ostensible reason for the First World War was because the Archduke Francis Ferdinand was assassinated.

CORRECT: The ostensible reason for the First World War was that the Archduke Francis Ferdinand was assassinated.

IMPROVED: The ostensible reason for the First World War was the assassination of the Archduke Francis Ferdinand.

Remember that *where* indicates location or position; it should not be used to introduce statements that do not concern position or location.

INCORRECT: Amnesia is where you lose your memory.

CORRECT: Amnesia occurs when you lose your memory.

IMPROVED: Amnesia is a loss of memory.

9

Comparison

9 A Adjectives and adverbs have three degrees:

THE POSITIVE DEGREE:	large	friendly	suitable
THE COMPARATIVE DEGREE:	larger	more friendly	more suitable
THE SUPERLATIVE DEGREE:	largest	most friendly	most suitable

9 B A few words have irregular comparative forms:

little, smaller, smallest [referring to size]
little, less, least [referring to degree or amount]
good, better, best [adjectives]
well, better, best [adverbs]
far, farther, farthest [referring to distance]
far, further, furthest [referring to degree or time]
much, more, most [referring to quantity (mass nouns)]
many, more, most [referring to quantity (count nouns)]
bad, worse, worst [adjectives]

9 C The comparative degree, not the superlative, is used when just two items are being compared.

David and Bill are both good sprinters, but I think Bill is *better*. [not *the best*]

9 D The superlative is used when three or more items are being compared.

Mary, Nancy, and Suzanne are trying out for the lead role. Each of them is good, but I think Nancy will get the part since she has had *the most* experience.   [not *more experience*]

---

9 E   Informal discourse sometimes allows a superlative when a comparative is technically required.

Which candidate, Turner or Norton, is *most* likely to support the needed housing legislation?

I've been to both Rome and London; I liked Rome *the best.*

---

9 F   Do not use a double comparative.

Incorrect:

Kenneth is a *more faster* runner than Kevin.

The sentence should read:

Kenneth is a faster runner than Kevin.

or

Kenneth is a much faster runner than Kevin.

---

9 G   Make sure that comparisons are not ambiguous. Instead of saying

I like you more than Anne.

be sure to clarify exactly what is being compared:

I like you more than Anne *does.*
I like you more than *I like* Anne.

---

9 H   Be sure that you use the correct case of pronouns in a comparison. The pronoun being compared should be in the same case as the word it is being compared to. If the

pronoun is being compared to the subject of the sentence, that pronoun should be in the subject case:

We like you more than *they*.

This sentence means *We like you more than they like you*.

If the pronoun is being compared to the object of the sentence, that pronoun should be in the objective case:

We like *you* more than *them*.

This sentence means *We like you more than we like them*.

---

9 I Be sure that you are comparing the precise words that you intend to compare. Note the following sentence:

Mrs. Dailey's professional expertise is greater than her husband.

Her expertise is not greater than her husband. Rather, her expertise is greater than her husband's expertise. What the speaker should have said is

Mrs. Dailey's professional expertise is greater than her *husband's*.

or

Mrs. Dailey's professional expertise is greater than *that of her husband*.

---

9 J Make sure that comparisons are logical. When you are comparing something to other members of the same class, make sure that you exclude the first item from the class by inserting the word *other* or *else*.

Illogical comparison:

London is larger than any city in England.

This sentence states that London is larger than all cities in England; since London is in England, this sentence illogically states that London is larger than London. What the speaker needs to do is to exclude London from the group of other cities in England:

London is larger than any *other* city in England.

Similarly, the sentence

The mayor is a better diplomat than anyone in the administration.

illogically states that the mayor is not a member of the administration. The sentence should read:

The mayor is a better diplomat than anyone *else* in the administration.

Note carefully the difference in meaning between the following two sentences:

Eleanor is a better speaker than *anyone* on the debating team.

Eleanor is a better speaker than *anyone else* on the debating team.

The first sentence says that Eleanor is not a member of the debating team. In the second sentence, however, Eleanor is a member of the debating team.

---

9 K   Make sure that comparisons are complete. Avoid omitting the object of the comparison, for such an omission can lead to confusion. For instance, note the following incomplete comparison:

Most owners vouch for the fact that Fords are better.

The reader wonders: better than what? Are Fords better now than they used to be? better than Cadillacs? better than having no car at all? better than other cars that owners have had?

---

9 L   When you use the word *more* in a comparison, make sure that its position in the sentence is precise. For instance, the position of *more* in the following sentence is misleading:

9 COMPARISON

More doctors prefer Crest.

This sentence can be interpreted in several ways—for instance:

More doctors than dentists prefer Crest.

More doctors prefer Crest nowadays than they did fifty years ago.

What that speaker actually wants to say is probably something like:

Doctors prefer Crest more than they prefer any other toothpaste.

or

Doctors prefer Crest to any other toothpaste.

---

9 M Make sure that comparisons do not omit essential words. For instance, *as* should be followed by another *as* to complete the comparison, and *as . . . as* is often complemented by *if not . . . than.*

Incomplete:

We are as competent, if not more competent than you.

The comparison should be completed:

We are as competent *as,* if not more competent *than,* you are.

But even the corrected sentence is awkward. It is much more natural to say

We are as competent as you are, if not more so.

---

9 N After a negative in a comparison, *as* is informal, *so* is formal.

FORMAL: You are not *so* clever as you think you are.

INFORMAL: You are not *as* clever as you think you are.

The informal construction is more natural than the formal.

10

Placement of Modifiers

A modifier is a word or a group of words that describes or qualifies another word or another group of words. All adjectives and adverbs are modifiers; similarly, all phrases and clauses that function as adjectives or adverbs are modifiers. In the following sentences, the modifiers are italicized and the word(s) being modified are in boldface type:

I have *just* **finished** *my* **report.**

People *who are rude* should be ignored.

He **pleaded** *his* **case** *with the skill of a professional.*

He pleaded *his* **case** *objectively and professionally.*

While visiting the United States, **Dvořak** collected *several Indian folk* **melodies** and incorporated them in one of *his* **symphonies.**

Caught in the trap, the *helpless* **animal suffered** *miserably.*

It is important that the position of modifiers be precise and unambiguous; otherwise, the sentence may be misleading or confusing.

MISPLACED MODIFIERS

10 A   A modifier should be as close as possible to the word(s) being modified; otherwise, the reader may be misled. Pay special care that words like *almost, hardly, scarcely, nearly, just, even, only* modify precisely the word(s) they are intended to modify.

MISLEADING: Jonas Salk only developed his vaccine for polio after many years of research.

Surely Dr. Salk did other things than develop a vaccine for polio.

IMPROVED: Jonas Salk developed his vaccine for polio only after many years of research.

It is the time that is being stressed, not the act of developing.

MISLEADING: Do you ever think that there will be peace between Israel and Iran?

IMPROVED: Do you think that there will ever be peace between Israel and Iran?

MISLEADING: Martin Luther King pleaded for the brotherhood of mankind in Mississippi.

IMPROVED: Martin Luther King pleaded in Mississippi for the brotherhood of mankind.

10 B   Another type of misplaced modifier occurs when the modifier can modify more than one element in the sentence. Such a modifier is called an **ambiguous modifier** or sometimes a **squinting modifier**.

AMBIGUOUS: I read three articles about defenestration in 1975.

Did you do the reading in 1975 or were the articles written in 1975 or did the acts of defenestration occur in 1975?

IMPROVED: In 1975 I read three articles about defenestration.

I read three articles written in 1975 about defenestration.

I read three articles about instances of defenestration that occurred in 1975.

AMBIGUOUS: The neighborhood newspaper prints announcements only in the weekend edition.

IMPROVED: The neighborhood newspaper prints only announcements in the weekend edition.

The neighborhood newspaper prints announcements in only the weekend edition.

Note the possible ambiguity in the following sentence:

I told my sister about the accident when I got home.

Because of the careless phrasing of this sentence, there are two possible interpretations:

When I got home, I told my sister about the accident.

I told my sister about the accident that occurred when I got home.

10 C   A relative pronoun should be as near to its antecedent as possible. Instead of saying:

The International Trade Commission is sending its best advisor to Washington, whom I hope to meet.

the speaker should have more clearly said:

The International Trade Commission is sending to Washington its best advisor, whom I hope to meet.

DANGLING MODIFIERS

A dangling modifier is one that does not have anything to modify . . . or at least that does not have anything that makes sense for it to modify. The word that it should be modifying has most likely been omitted or implied. It is called *dangling* because, not having anything to modify, its connection with the rest of the sentence is loose.

---

10 D One way to correct a dangling modifier is to insert a specific subject into the modifier and then to have the verb agree with that subject.

DANGLING: While on vacation, our house was burglarized.

This sentence incorrectly states that our house was on vacation.

CORRECTED: While *we were* on vacation, our house was burglarized.

DANGLING: In order to succeed, perseverance is necessary.

CORRECTED: *If you want* to succeed, perserverance is necessary.

DANGLING: His chief strength is music, having given several performances during the past year.

CORRECTED: His chief strength is music, *and he has given* several performances during the past year.

---

10 E Another way to correct a dangling modifier is to rephrase the sentence so that the modifier does indeed modify the appropriate word.

DANGLING: In order to succeed, perseverance is necessary.

CORRECTED: In order to succeed, *you must have* perseverance.

DANGLING: This year Terry's grade-point average improved by five points, doing his best work in history.

CORRECTED: This year *Terry improved* his grade-point average by five points, doing his best work in history.

DANGLING: Pressured by an irate populace who would not tolerate any new taxes, the Jarvis proposal seemed like a good idea.

CORRECTED: Pressured by an irate populace who would not tolerate any new taxes, *the administration sponsored (accepted, supported)* the Jarvis proposal.

11

Verbs

A few references to verbs have already appeared in earlier chapters, and these references should be reviewed: the principles of agreement between subject and verb (Chapter 3) and the selection of modifiers after verbs of the senses and verbs of being (Sections 8 A through 8 E). The properties of verbs are summarized on pages 58–59.

THE SELECTION OF TENSES

By and large, we select our tenses automatically and naturally. We know that if we wish to talk about something that is happening at the time of our speaking, we will use the present tense. We know that if we wish to talk about something that will happen, we use the future tense. And we naturally use a past tense if we want to talk about something that has already occurred. But, whereas we are usually precise in our use of the present and future tenses, we are often not as precise in our use of the past tense. The reason for such imprecision is simple: there are several different types of past tenses, and we are sometimes not sensitive to the differences among them. Therefore, it is worthwhile to itemize the different types of past tenses and to differentiate among them.

There is the **progressive past,** called the **imperfect** in some languages. This tense denotes continuous or repeated action in past time, and it is a tense used for vivid-

Verbs: Standard Terminology

Term	Description	Examples
Verb form	any part of a verb	go, going, went, gone
Number	whether the verb is singular or plural	is/are, was/were, has/have, goes/go, sees/see
Person	first person: the subject is *I* or *we*	I see, I was seen, I saw, we see, we were seen, we saw, we will see
	second person: the subject is *you*	you see, you saw, you have seen, you have been seen, you will be seen
	third person: the subject is a noun or a pronoun other than *I, we,* or *you*	war has been declared, she is coming, they are coming, the mayor says
Voice	active voice: the subject does the action	I am going, I saw, we have helped, we rescued
	passive voice: the action is done to the subject	I was seen, we have been helped, we were rescued
	(Note: the verb *be* is neither active nor passive. It merely denotes a state of being.)	
Tense	the time of the action of the verb:	
	present tense	I run, I am running, we are being helped
	present perfect	I have run, I have been running, he has fled, they have been helped
	simple past (completed past)	I ran, we aided, they fled
	progressive past	I was running, we were aiding, we used to run, they were being aided
	past perfect	I had run, I had been running, they had been helped
	future	I will run, I will be running, he will flee, they shall survive
	future perfect	I will have run, I will have been running, he will have fled, they will have been helped

Term	Description	Examples
Mood *Finite forms*	indicative mood: states a fact or asks a question	I was going Are you willing?
	subjunctive mood: indicates an idea, a wish, or an impossibility	(if) I were you
	imperative mood: states a command or request	Go! Be gone!
Verbals	infinitive: a verb preceded by the word *to*	to help, to be helped, to have helped, to have been helped
	participle: a verb form used as an adjective	(while) helping, (while) being helped, (having) helped, (having been) helped
	gerund: a verb form used as a noun	helping, being helped
Auxiliary verb	a verb form that helps to indicate the tense, mood, person, or number of a verb	we *might* go, we *will* go, we *were being* helped, we *have been* helped
Verb phrase	a verb with its auxiliaries	we *might go,* we *will go,* they *were being helped,* she *has been helped*
Finite verb	a complete verb form — a combination of subject and finite verb constitutes a complete sentence	we *saw,* we *were being seen,* we *might see,* I *might have been seen*
Transitive verb	a verb that takes a direct object	I *ran* the campaign.
Intransitive verb	a verb that does not take a direct object	I *ran* into the building.
Agreement	the aligning of the verb with its subject so that a singular subject will take a singular verb and a plural subject will take a plural verb	The house is/was/has been The houses are/were/have been
Regular verb	a verb whose past tense is predictable (ends in *-d* or *-ed*)	walk – walked help – helped
Irregular verb	a verb whose past tense is not predictable (does not add *-d* or *-ed* to the present tense)	go – gone see – saw

ness, liveliness, and action. There are various forms for the progressive past:

ACTIVE VOICE: I was training, I used to train, I kept on training, I did train

PASSIVE VOICE: I was trained, I was being trained, I used to be trained, I kept on being trained

There is the **simple past** tense, sometimes called the **definite past.** This tense stresses the finality of an action or event—as opposed to the progressive past, which stresses the continuity of an action or of an event.

ACTIVE VOICE: I trained

PASSIVE VOICE: I was trained

The **present perfect** tense, in some languages called merely the **perfect** tense, indicates an action or event that began in the past but has continued up to the time of speaking and is completed at the time of speaking. For instance, the present perfect *I have arrived* is very close to the present *I am here.* Whereas the progressive past stresses continuity in the past, the present perfect stresses continuity from past to present and the completion of the action.

ACTIVE VOICE: I have trained, I have been training

PASSIVE VOICE: I have been trained

The **past perfect** tense, often called the **pluperfect** tense in other languages, expresses a relationship between one event and another. The past perfect indicates that one action or event in the past occurred before some other action or event that also occurred in the past. Since the past perfect tense expresses a relationship between two past acts, it rarely stands alone in a sentence.

ACTIVE VOICE: I had trained, I had been training

PASSIVE VOICE: I had been trained

SINGLE ACT IN THE PAST: Europe *was* at war.

RELATIONSHIP BETWEEN TWO PAST ACTS: Europe *had been* at war for several years before the United States entered the conflict.

11 A   If a main verb is in a past tense and you want to express another action that occurred before the time of that main verb, use the past perfect tense.

I wondered where everyone *had gone.*   [not *went*]

The main verb *wondered* is in the past tense. The second verb expresses another action that has already occurred. Therefore, that second verb should be in the past perfect tense.

The following sentence illustrates a very common error:

After we drove for a few miles, we realized that we were on the wrong road.

Since we did the driving before we did the realizing, the two acts did not happen simultaneously. Therefore, *drove* should have been put in the past perfect tense:

After we *had driven* for several miles, we realized that we were on the wrong road.

or

After we *had been driving* for several miles, we realized that we were on the wrong road.

---

11 B   If a main verb is in a past tense and you want to express another action that is happening at the same time, use the progressive past.

I wondered where everyone *was going.*

Since the war in Europe *was having* effects upon the American economy, government officials realized that America could not remain neutral for much longer.

While we *were driving* from San Francisco to Los Angeles, we saw three serious accidents.

---

11 C   A statement that expresses a general truth — for example, one that is as true now as it was when the statement was

originally made—can be in the present tense even if the main verb is in the past.

Socrates believed that humans *differ* from other animals in that humans *are* rational.

Humans still differ from other animals in that humans are still rational.

---

11 D   Care must be exercised in the selection of auxiliary verbs. After a present, a future, or a present perfect tense, use *can, will, shall, may.* After a verb in the past tense, use *could, would, should, might.*

I think this *may* [not *might*] be just what I have been looking for.

The President announced that he *would* [not *will*] take severe measures to curb inflation.

If the future time is specific, however, the primary forms *(will, can, may, shall)* are used:

The President announced that *next week* he *will* take severe measures to combat inflation.

---

11 E   The present perfect introduces a present, not a past tense.

I *have believed* for a long time that the war *is* an unjust one.

as opposed to

I *believed* for a long time that the war *was* an unjust one.

---

11 F   The future tense merely expresses an event in the future. The future perfect, on the other hand, expresses a relationship between that future event and another future event that will occur before that first future event has been accomplished.

FUTURE: I will visit Scandinavia this summer.

FUTURE PERFECT: Before the summer is over, I will have visited Scandinavia.

VERBALS

A verbal is a verb form used as some other part of speech. The easiest verbal to recognize is the infinitive: *to* followed by a verb—*to see, to be seen, to have seen, to have been seen.* The other two types of verbals are gerunds and participles. They often look alike, but they differ in their function within a sentence. The gerund functions like a noun (see Section 6 I), whereas the participle functions like an adjective.

PARTICIPLE: Seeing the accident, we became very upset.

GERUND: Seeing the accident made us very upset.

PARTICIPLE: Being informed that there were several radar traps on the road, we drove within the speed limit.

GERUND: Being informed that there were several radar traps on the road prompted us to drive within the speed limit.

PARTICIPLE: Having been insulted in public, I vowed revenge.

GERUND: Having been insulted in public made me vow revenge.

---

11 G Grammarians used to fuss over split infinitives—that is, over putting a word or words between the *to* and the verb form. Nowadays, split infinitives are acceptable especially if the split helps to avoid clumsiness, unnaturalness, or ambiguity.

I want *to* truly *thank* Thatcher and Adam for their assistance.

But one should still avoid a long split between the *to* and the verb.

Unacceptable split:

I tried *to,* by examining all the evidence, *determine* whether there was any precedent.

Improved:

I tried, by examining all the evidence, to determine whether there was any precedent.

---

11 H The tense of an infinitive is determined by the verb upon which the infinitive depends. The present infinitive expresses an action that occurs at the same time as the action of the main verb; the past infinitive expresses an action that has occurred before the action of the main verb.

INCORRECT: I preferred *to have been called* by my first name.
CORRECT: I preferred *to be called* by my first name.

The act of preferring and the act of calling are occurring at the same time; therefore, the present infinitive should be used.

INCORRECT: I am sorry *to miss* your recital.
CORRECT: I am sorry *to have missed* your recital.

Since I miss the recital before I am sorry, the past infinitive should be used.

---

11 I Be sure to use a possessive in front of a gerund. (See Section 6 I for other examples.)

I resent Judy's [not *Judy*] always trying to find excuses.

You do not resent Judy; you resent her tendency to find excuses.

---

11 J When selecting a participle, be sure to choose the right tense. Use the present participle only when the action expressed by that participle is occurring at the same time as the action of the main verb.

Fleeing from my assailant, I sprained my ankle.

Similarly, use the past participle only when the action expressed by that participle has occurred before the action expressed by the main verb.

Having fled from my assailant, I filed a full report of the incident with the police.

The following sentence illustrates a common error:

Witnessing the crime, I was asked to testify.

Since I had to witness before I could be asked to testify, the two acts are not occurring simultaneously; therefore, the present participle *witnessing* is inaccurate. The past participle should be used:

Having witnessed the crime, I was asked to testify.

VOICE

The voice of a verb specifies whether the subject of a sentence is the doer or the receiver of an action. There are two voices: the active voice, in which the subject does the action, and the passive voice, in which the action is done to the subject or in which the subject is affected by the action.

ACTIVE: I *witnessed* the court-martial.

PASSIVE: The court-martial *was witnessed* by me.

ACTIVE: Michelangelo *painted* the ceiling of the Sistine Chapel.

PASSIVE: The ceiling of the Sistine Chapel *was painted* by Michelangelo.

ACTIVE: Michelangelo's monumental painting in the Sistine Chapel *has delighted* and *impressed* thousands of people.

PASSIVE: Thousands of people *have been delighted* and *impressed* by Michelangelo's painting in the Sistine Chapel.

11 K   The passive voice is weaker, less forceful, and more vague than the active voice. It should be used sparingly. It can be used when the writer wants to stress the recipient of the action rather than the doer of the action.

The word "cryptic" is derived from the Greek root "krupt-," which means "concealed" or "hidden"; hence, a cryptic remark is one whose true meaning *is concealed* or *hidden.*

The passive voice encourages impersonality and matter-of-factness. Therefore, if vividness and action are being denoted, the passive voice is both inappropriate and ineffective.

MATTER-OF-FACT: On June 25, 1876, George A. Custer was attacked by a swarm of Sioux Indians, and he and his men were summarily annihilated.

VIVID: On June 25, 1876, a swarm of Sioux Indians attacked and summarily annihilated George A. Custer and his men.

The passive voice is fine where the object of the action is the focus rather than the doer of the action, as in much scientific and technical writing:

Energy cannot *be* either *created* or *destroyed;* it can merely *be redirected* and *transformed.* This principle *is known* as the law of the conservation of energy. It *was* first *cited* by Mayer in the mid-nineteenth century and later *expanded* by Joule and Einstein.

THE SUBJUNCTIVE MOOD

Whereas the indicative mood makes a statement or asks a question, the subjunctive mood expresses a wish, an idea, or an impossibility:

INDICATIVE: I was going

SUBJUNCTIVE: (if) I were going

The subjunctive mood was once used much more extensively than it is used now. Most of the former uses of the subjunctive have become absorbed by the indicative. In fact, only the present and the past subjunctives have distinct forms that are used anymore. The present subjunctive of a verb is the infinitive of that verb without the *to*. The following illustrates the conjugation of the present subjunctive of the verb *be* and of the verb *ask:*

I be	we be	I ask	we ask
you be	you be	you ask	you ask
he be	they be	he ask	they ask

Only the verb *be* uses distinct forms of the past subjunctive:

I were	we were
you were	you were
he were	they were

In spite of its relative rarity, however, the subjunctive is used in a few important constructions.

---

11 L The present subjunctive is used in a subordinate clause to indicate an action that is necessary or required.

It is necessary that he *leave* at once.

I insist that you *be* accurate in your computation.

Mr. Bingham requested that we all *be* present for this meeting.

---

11 M The past subjunctive expresses a wish.

If only he *were* here!

I wish that he *were* here.

---

11 N The subjunctive is also used in a condition that cannot be a fact.

If I *were* you, I would not have made those remarks.

(But I am not you and I never will be.)

If it *were* not raining, we would not have to postpone our trip.

(But it is raining, and there's nothing we can do about it.)

11 VERBS

MISCELLANEOUS

11 O   Never use *of* after *could, should, would, might, may, will, shall, must.* Always use *have.*

You should *have* arrived earlier.

11 P   Introduce an indirect statement with *that,* not *as* or *where.*

I heard *that* [not *where* or *as*] there has been a recent eruption of hostility in the Middle East.

11 Q   The following verbs are nuisances. Either avoid using them or else use them correctly.

a) *Lie:* to tell a falsehood

I lie   I am lying   I lied   I have lied

b) *Lie:* to rest, to be situated

I lie down   I am lying down   earlier I lay down
I have lain down

c) *Lay:* to put or place

I lay the package down   I am laying the package down
I laid the package down   I have laid the package down

11 R   There are many verbs that are often used incorrectly or are often confused with another word. If you are uncertain about how any of the following words are used, check the glossary of usage, Chapter 37.

accept	affect	effect	aggravate
can	may	compare	contrast
precede	proceed	raise	rise
sit	set	bring	take

11 S A contraction is a word formed from the merging of two words. At the point of contraction, a letter is omitted. An apostrophe is inserted *where this letter is omitted.*

do not – don't	are not – aren't	did not – didn't
who is – who's	they are – they're	I am – I'm
we are – we're	was not – wasn't	will not – won't
it is – it's	is not – isn't	should not – shouldn't

11 T The past tense of a verb is usually formed by adding *-ed* or *-d* to the verb:

believe – believed   aid – aided   call – called

The past participle of these verbs is identical to the past tense.

PAST TENSE: I *believed* in him until I discovered he was a fraud.

PAST PARTICIPLE: *Having believed* in him for so long, I was upset when I discovered he was a fraud.

11 U But there are many verbs whose past tense is irregular and whose past participle is not necessarily the same as their past tense. The list on pages 70 – 71 cites most of the important irregular verbs together with their past tense and their past participle; the present participle is also included to contrast with the past participle. If you are not sure of the principal parts of a verb that is not included in this list, by all means consult a dictionary.

Principal Parts of Irregular Verbs

Present	Past	Present participle	Past participle
arise	arose	arising	arisen
ask	asked	asking	asked
awake	awoke *or* awaked	awaking	awoke *or* awaked
bear	bore	bearing	borne
beat	beat	beating	beaten
begin	began	beginning	begun
bend	bent	bending	bent
bind	bound	binding	bound
bite	bit	biting	bitten
blow	blew	blowing	blown
break	broke	breaking	broken
bring	brought	bringing	brought
build	built	building	built
burn	burned *or* burnt	burning	burned *or* burnt
buy	bought	buying	bought
cast	cast	casting	cast
catch	caught	catching	caught
choose	chose	choosing	chosen
come	came	coming	come
cost	cost	costing	cost
deal	dealt	dealing	dealt
dive	dived *or* dove	diving	dived *or* dove
draw	drew	drawing	drawn
drink	drank	drinking	drunk
dream	dreamed *or* dreamt	dreaming	dreamed *or* dreamt
drive	drove	driving	driven
drown	drowned	drowning	drowned
eat	ate	eating	eaten
fall	fell	falling	fallen
forbid	forbade	forbidding	forbidden
forget	forgot	forgetting	forgotten
freeze	froze	freezing	frozen
get	got	getting	gotten *or* got
give	gave	giving	given
go	went	going	gone
grow	grew	growing	grown
have	had	having	had
hear	heard	hearing	heard
hide	hid	hiding	hidden
hit	hit	hitting	hit
know	knew	knowing	known
lead	led	leading	led

Present	Past	Present participle	Past participle
lend	lent	lending	lent
leap	leaped *or* leapt	leaping	leaped *or* leapt
learn	learned *or* learnt	learning	learned *or* learnt
light	lighted *or* lit	lighting	lighted *or* lit
loose	loosed	loosening	loosed
pay	paid	paying	paid
prove	proved	proving	proved *or* proven
raise	raised	raising	raised
read	read	reading	read
ride	rode	riding	ridden
ring	rang	ringing	rung
rise	rose	rising	risen
run	ran	running	run
say	said	saying	said
see	saw	seeing	seen
seek	sought	seeking	sought
sew	sewed	sewing	sewed *or* sown
shake	shook	shaking	shaken
show	showed	showing	shown *or* showed
sing	sang	singing	sung
sink	sank	sinking	sunk
sit	sat	sitting	sat
slide	slid	sliding	slid *or* slidden
sneak	sneaked	sneaking	sneaked
speak	spoke	speaking	spoken
spend	spent	spending	spent
spin	spun	spinning	spun
stay	stayed	staying	stayed
steal	stole	stealing	stolen
stick	stuck	sticking	stuck
stink	stank *or* stunk	stinking	stunk
strike	struck	striking	struck *or* stricken
strive	strove	striving	striven *or* strived
suppose	supposed	supposing	supposed
sweep	swept	sweeping	swept
swim	swam	swimming	swum
swing	swung	swinging	swung
take	took	taking	taken
teach	taught	teaching	taught
tear	tore	tearing	torn
throw	threw	throwing	thrown
try	tried	trying	tried
wake	waked *or* woke	waking	waked
wear	wore	wearing	worn
win	won	winning	won
wring	wrung	wringing	wrung
write	wrote	writing	written

12

Conjunctions and Prepositions

This is a chapter on little words, words that express connection (conjunctions) and words that indicate relationship (prepositions). If a sentence does not express the precise connection that the writer intends to express or if a word does not indicate the specific relationship that the writer intends to indicate, the reader may be confused and misled. Selecting the right conjunction or preposition will assist the writer in communicating exactly what he wants to say.

---

12 A   Do not repeat the conjunction *that* when it is separated from the word(s) it governs, even if that separation is a long one.

> INCORRECT: We all hope *that,* after the scandal has been forgotten and after responsible leadership has been reinstated, *that* harmony will again prevail throughout the land.

One *that* should be deleted.

---

12 B   But do repeat the *that* when it introduces two or more parallel ideas.

We all hope *that* harmony will again prevail throughout the land and *that* people will again begin to trust their leaders.

12 C   After an expression of doubt, use *that* (not *but that*) and *whether* (not *if*).

> I don't doubt *that* [not *but that*] the twenty-first century will see massive technological dependency.
>
> There is no doubt *that* [not *but that*] the twenty-first century will become heavily dependent upon technology.
>
> World leaders doubt *whether* [not *if*] global peace will ever be achieved.

12 D   Use *whether* to introduce an indirect question.

> Freud sometimes wondered *whether* his theories would ever be accepted by his colleagues.

12 E   *Whether* and *if* should not be used interchangeably in introducing subordinate clauses. When you can insert the words *or not* or when you can insert the conjunction *or*, introduce the clause with *whether*. In other words, use *whether* when there are alternatives.

> We speculated *whether (or not)* she would arrive on time.
>
> I did not know *whether* the allusion was to Shakespeare *or* to Milton.

But when there are no alternatives, use *if*.

> I wonder what would happen *if* China were to attack Russia.

In this sentence, one cannot insert *or not* or *or:* therefore, *whether* would be inaccurate. The sentence expresses a simple condition; there are no alternatives.

12 F   Use a gerund, not *but*, after the expression *cannot help*.

> We couldn't help *wondering* [not *but wonder*] what it would be like to lead the life of a celebrity.

12 CONJUNCTIONS AND PREPOSITIONS

12 G   Be careful when using the word *since;* it can sometimes have ambiguous meanings.

Since I broke my leg, I understand what it is like to be disabled.

The *since* in this sentence can be regarded as *ever since* or as *because;* in the former case, it expresses time; in the latter case, it expresses cause. Rather than risk ambiguity, use *ever since* when you wish to express time and use *because* when you wish to express causation.

---

12 H   *Being that, being as,* and *seeing as how* are weak. Instead, use the straightforward word *because.*

Because we are becoming too dependent upon foreign sources for our requirements of oil, we must work to secure our own supplies.

---

12 I   Do not write *as* when you mean *because. As* indicates time, not consequence.

INCORRECT: As I was late, I began to speed.

CORRECT: Because I was late, I began to speed.

CORRECT: As I was driving, my mind began to wander.

---

12 J   Avoid the formula *is because, is where, is when.* (See Section 8 H.)

---

12 K   Use *different than* only when a clause follows—that is, when a group of words with both a subject and verb follows.

The movie was different than I had expected it to be.

Otherwise use *different from.*

The movie was different from what I had expected.

A solution is different *from* [not *than*] a mixture. The two words should not be used interchangeably.

---

12 L   Distinguish between *like* and *as. Like* is a preposition; it can be substituted by *similar to. As* is a conjunction; it connects clauses; it can usually be substituted by *in the way that.*

If you behave (like/as) a boor, you will not gain respect.

First of all, *a boor* is not a clause; secondly, *in the way that* cannot be substituted. On the other hand, *a boor* is appropriately introduced by a preposition; secondly, *similar to* can be substituted. Therefore, the correct word is *like,* the preposition.

If you do only (like/as) you wish, your behavior will be regarded as narcissistic.

First of all, *you wish* is a clause, since it contains a subject and a verb; second, the words *similar to* cannot be substituted but the words *in the way that* can certainly be substituted. Therefore, the correct word is *as,* the conjunction.

---

12 M   *As* is not a preposition. Do not use it when the preposition *like* or *such as* is needed.

INCORRECT: Even outstanding actors *as* Bette Davis have made a few bad films.

CORRECT: Even outstanding actors *such as* [or *like*] Bette Davis have made a few bad films.

12 N   Don't use the preposition *like* when the conjunction *as if* is needed.

It sounded *as if* [not *like*] the whole police force had been summoned.

12 O   Remember to express the complete form of the comparison *as . . . as, if not . . . than, ...*

The invention of the gasoline engine is *as* important *as, if not* more important *than,* the discovery of electricity.

or

The invention of the gasoline engine is as important as the discovery of electricity, if not more so.

12 P   Don't use double prepositions. In particular, don't use the prepositions *of* or *with* when they are not necessary.

They are inside the building.   [not *inside of the building*]
The barrels fell off the platform.   [not *off of the platform*]
The play is over.   [not *over with*]

12 Q   In formal writing, use an infinitive after *try* and after *plan.*

Try *to finish* on time.   [not *Try and finish on time.*]
Plan *to get* here early.   [not *Plan on getting here early.*]

12 R   Words of emotion often require a preposition to complete the meaning. When there is a choice among prepositions, usually the preposition *with* applies to people.

to agree *with* a person	to agree *in* our attitudes to agree *on* what to do to agree *to* an idea
to be angry *with* a person	to be angry *at* an act or a thing
to be annoyed *with* a person	to be annoyed *at* an act or a thing
to argue *with* a person	to argue *for/against* a proposal
to concur *with* a person	to concur *in* our decision, idea, opinion
to confer *with* a person	to confer *about* a proposal

---

12 S   The following list cites some of the idiomatic uses of prepositions:

to blame someone *for* something   [not *to blame something on someone*]

to acquaint yourself *with* the information   [not *of the information*]

to compare X *to* Y = to cite similarities between X and Y

to compare X *with* Y = to cite both similarities and differences

to contrast X *with* Y = to cite differences between X and Y

a contrast *between* X and Y

in contrast *to*

to comprise (followed by no preposition)   [not *to be comprised of*]

X comprises A, B, C, and D.

to be concerned *about* = to be worried, uneasy about

We are concerned about the condition of the economy.

to be concerned *with* = to be interested in
We are concerned with your welfare.

correspond *to* = be similar to

correspond *with* = write letters to

differ *in* = have different
We differ in our estimates. = We have different estimates.

differ *from* = be different from
Impressionism differs from expressionism.

differ *with* = disagree with
I differ with you. = I disagree with you.

equally (followed by no preposition) [not *equally as*]
Football and hockey are not equally violent.

forbid *to*   [not *forbid from*]
I was forbidden to take the car last night.

independent *of*   [not *independent from*]

identical *with*   [not *identical to*]

to be optimistic/pessimistic *about*   [not *to be optimistic/pessimistic that*]

prefer X *to/over/above* Y   [not *prefer X than Y*]

prejudiced *against*   [not *prejudiced toward*]

superior *to*   [not *superior than*]

talk *to* = inform, reprimand
I'll have to talk to him about that.

talk *with* = chat, confer, discuss

13

Coordination and Balance

In order to avoid writing a series of short choppy sentences, writers will often want to express connection among their ideas and to show the relationship between one idea and another. The joining of ideas equal in importance is called coordination; the word used to join these ideas is a coordinate conjunction, such as *and, but, or, for, nor.*

The coordinate conjunction can join single words:

The pre-Socratic philosophers believed that there were four basic elements: water, air, earth, and fire.

or groups of words:

The pre-Socratic philosophers believed that there were four basic elements and that one of these elements dominated the others.

or complete sentences:

The pre-Socratic philosophers believed that there were four basic elements, but they differed about the relative importance of these elements.

SIMPLE COORDINATION

13 A   When writing a sentence in which you wish to express coordination — that is, in which you use conjunctions such

as *and, or, nor, as well as, but* — be sure that the elements being joined are similar. In other words, a verb should be joined with another verb, a noun with another noun, a prepositional phrase with another prepositional phrase, an adjective with another adjective, a clause with a similar clause, and so on. If the elements are not similar, the sentence will be imbalanced and hence will sound lopsided; furthermore, the sentence may be unclear and illogical. Similar elements are often called **parallel elements.** To combine dissimilar elements is often called **faulty parallelism.**

IMBALANCED: He told the people of his adventures and that he was now ready to assume the throne.

He told the people
⟋ of his adventures
⟍ and
that he was now ready to assume the throne.

A prepositional phrase is improperly being joined with a clause. Here is one way to balance this sentence:

He told the people of his adventures
and
he assured them that he was now ready to assume the throne.

The *and* is now joining two verbs: *he told* and *he assured.*

ILLOGICAL: Members of the seminar will be required to conduct a class as well as preparing an extended research paper.

Members of the seminar will be required
⟋ to conduct a class
⟍ as well as
preparing an extended research paper.

To conduct is improperly being joined with *preparing.* Balance can be easily achieved:

Members of the seminar will be required
⟋ to conduct a class
⟍ as well as
to prepare an extended research paper.

Now *to conduct* is properly being joined with *to prepare,* both infinitives.

---

13 B The same principles of balance should be employed when items in a series are joined.

IMBALANCED: The poetry of e e cummings uses irregular typography, punctuation, and expresses disapproval toward our mechanized approach to life.

The poetry of e e cummings uses
- irregular typography
- punctuation
- and
- expresses disapproval toward our mechanized approach to life.

BALANCED: The poetry of e e cummings uses irregular typography, has unconventional punctuation, and expresses disapproval toward our mechanized approach to life.

The poetry of e e cummings
- uses irregular typography
- has unconventional punctuation
- and
- expresses disapproval toward our mechanized approach to life.

or

The poetry of e e cummings uses irregular typography and punctuation and expresses disapproval toward our mechanized approach to life.

The poetry of e e cummings
- uses irregular typography and punctuation
- and
- expresses disapproval toward our mechanized approach to life.

The various elements in a series should be structurally similar: all nouns, or all verbs, or all prepositional phrases, or all introduced by the same word or the same type of word.

---

13 C   **Be sure to express the full form of a verb phrase, particularly when that verb phrase is not at the end of a sentence.**

INCOMPLETE: I always have and always will be loyal to the Constitution.

I   always have and always will be → loyal to the Constitution.

COMPLETE: I always have *been* and always will be loyal to the Constitution.

I   always have been and always will be → loyal to the Constitution.

or

I have always been loyal to the Constitution and always will be.

---

13 D   **Be sure to include all the necessary prepositions.**

INCOMPLETE: I was interested and pleased by your remarks.

I was   interested and pleased → by your remarks.

The sentence incorrectly states: *I was interested by your remarks.* The writer should have inserted the appropriate preposition after *interested.*

COMPLETE: I was interested *in* and pleased by your remarks.

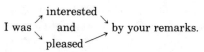

I was   interested in and pleased by → your remarks.

13 E   *And* or *but* should not immediately be followed by a relative pronoun unless the relative pronoun has appeared at least once before in the sentence.

> INCORRECT: Lucie Manette was a gentle soul *and who* spoke kindly of everyone.
>
> CORRECT: Lucie Manette was a gentle soul *who* spoke kindly of everyone.
>
> CORRECT: Lucie Manette was a gentle soul *who* spoke kindly of everyone *and who* believed in all that is good.

INCORRECT: A cultured person is one appreciating the arts but who can distinguish art from sham.

appreciating the arts

A cultured person is one   but

who can distinguish art from sham.

> CORRECT: A cultured person is one *who appreciates* the arts but *who can distinguish* art from sham.

---

13 F   Be sure that comparisons are properly balanced—that is, that you are comparing the elements that you intend to compare. (See also Section 9 I.)

> FAULTY: Rubinstein's renditions of Chopin's piano music are not as exciting as Horowitz.

This sentence improperly compares *renditions* with *Horowitz.*

> IMPROVED: Rubinstein's renditions of Chopin's piano music are not as exciting as Horowitz's.

Now the sentence properly compares Rubinstein's renditions with Horowitz's renditions.

---

13 G   Be sure that parallel items are expressed from the same point of view. For instance, in the following sentence:

The newly appointed Secretary of the Treasury promises to identify, improve, and solve the economic problems that are besetting the country.

While it is possible that the Secretary will be able to identify and to solve the economic problems, by only a twisting of logic can one say that he or she will *improve* those problems. The point of view can be clarified:

The newly appointed Secretary of the Treasury promises to identify the economic problems, to solve those problems, and *to improve the economic conditions* of this country.

Here is another example:

As I listened to the lecture, I got irritable, restless, angry, and a stiff jab from my wife, who thought my behavior was rude.

In the first part of the sentence, the verb *got* is equivalent to *became;* in the second part, however, it changes its meaning to *receive.* The two different uses of the verb should be distinguished:

As I listened to the lecture, I got irritable, restless, and angry, and I received a stiff jab from my wife, who thought my behavior was rude.

---

13 H When you begin a particular kind of structure in a sentence, do not change that structure within the sentence. For instance, the sentence:

Mrs. Proudie said that it was time for her to leave and would I please call a cab.

establishes the structure *said that* but then alters that structure with the words *would I please:*

Mrs. Proudie said
- that it was time for her to leave
- and
- would I please call a cab.

There are several ways to balance the sentence. The two thoughts can be completely separated:

Mrs. Proudie said, "It is time to leave. Please call me a cab."

or coordination can be expressed between the two thoughts:

Mrs. Proudie *said* that it was time for her to leave and *asked* me to call a cab.

or

Mrs. Proudie said *that* it was time for her to leave and *that* I should call a cab.

---

13 I The final sentence in the section above illustrates a very important detail. When a word introduces two or more parallel ideas, it is usually wise to repeat that introductory word (or an equivalent of it).

Mrs. Proudie said *that* it was time for her to leave and *that* I should call a cab.

Mrs. Proudie said *that* it was time for her to leave, *that* she had had a fine time, and *that* she looked forward to several visits in the weeks ahead.

Mrs. Proudie said that is was time for her to leave and *she asked* me to call a cab.

Note how the repetition of an introductory word alters the meaning of the following sentence:

a) Mr. Guth said that he would call a meeting of all those students who want to learn to cook and form a cooking club.

b) Mr. Guth said that he would call a meeting of all those students who want to learn to cook and *who want to* form a cooking club.

c) Mr. Guth said that he would call a meeting of all those students who want to learn to cook and *that he would* form a cooking club.

In sentence (a), the *and* expresses ambiguous connection. Is it joining *form* with *cook, form* with *learn,* or *form* with *call?* By repeating the necessary introductory words, the sentences (b) and (c) remove the ambiguity.

13 COORDINATION AND BALANCE

The most common types of introductory words that often need to be repeated are the following:

1) prepositions

2) *to* when it introduces an infinitive

3) auxiliary verbs—tense or mood indicators, like *may, should, can, could, might, would, will, has, had, have, is, are, were*

4) the introductory word of a clause, such as *that, who, when, which, what, why, where, while, since, after, because, although, if*

5) a limiting adjective, such as *some, a, an, the, any*

6) a possessive adjective, such as *his, her, my, your, our, their*

Additional examples:

a) Mr. Greene thanked the people who had helped him and prepared a superb banquet.

b) Mr. Greene thanked the people who had helped him and *who had* prepared a superb banquet.

c) Mr. Greene thanked the people who had helped him, and *he* prepared a superb banquet.

In the first sentence the reader is unable to tell who prepared the banquet, Mr. Greene or the people who helped him. The second and third sentences are more precise.

a) There will be a 30 percent reduction on short-sleeve sport shirts and dress shirts.

b) There will be a 30 percent reduction on short-sleeve sport shirts and *on short-sleeve* dress shirts.

c) There will be a 30 percent reduction on short-sleeve sport shirts and *on all* dress shirts.

It is difficult to tell from the first sentence just what kind of shirts are on sale. The second and third sentences remove the ambiguity.

CORRELATIVE CONJUNCTIONS

13 J   Sometimes conjunctions are used in pairs. These are
        called correlative conjunctions. The most common correl-
        ative conjunctions are

both . . . and   either . . . or
not . . . but   neither . . . nor
not only . . . but also   whether . . . or

The same principles about coordination cited earlier in
this chapter apply to correlative conjunctions: if there is a
noun after the first conjunction, there should be a noun
after the second conjunction; if there is a prepositional
phrase after the first conjunction, there should be a prepositional phrase after the second conjunction. In other
words, the same type of element should be used after the
second conjunction as was used after the first.

Note how the following expressions must be balanced:

a) I both believe in them and . . .   (Another verb must follow.)

I both believe in them and trust them completely.

b) I believe both in them and . . .   (Another prepositional
                                        phrase must follow.)

I believe both in them and in their methods.

I believe both in them and in you.

c) I believe in both them and . . .   (An object must follow.)

I believe in both them and you.

I believe in both them and their methods.

d) He not only is clumsy but also . . . (Another verb must follow.)

He not only is clumsy but also always makes mistakes.

e) He is not only clumsy but also . . . (An adjective must follow.)

He is not only clumsy but also careless.

f) Not only is he clumsy but . . . (Another subject and verb are required.)

Not only is he clumsy but he is also always making mistakes.

g) He is not only a fool but also . . . (Another noun is required.)

He is not only a fool but also a clown.

h) He likes not only to go fishing but also . . . (Another infinitive phrase is needed.)

He likes not only to go fishing but also to build model planes.

i) I both want to visit Paris and . . .

Another verb is needed. But even when that verb is supplied, the sentence will still be clumsy and will probably not say what the speaker intended. What the speaker most likely intended is

I want both to visit Paris and . . . (Now another infinitive phrase is required.)

I want both to visit Paris and to travel to North Africa.

or

I want to visit both Paris and . . . (Now a noun is required.)

I want to visit both Paris and North Africa.

j) Note the improper balance in the following sentence:

I neither believe in you nor in your methods.

A verb is following the first conjunction and a prepositional
phrase follows the second conjunction. Balance may be restored
in the following ways:

I neither believe in you nor trust your methods.

I believe neither in you nor in your methods.

I believe in neither you nor your methods.

IMPROPER COORDINATION

13 K   Only thoughts that are relatively equal in importance
should be coordinated. Furthermore, the reason for the
joining of those ideas should be clear. Writers should be
particularly careful not to join unrelated ideas by the conjunction *and*.

> PROPER: The reign of Queen Elizabeth brought to England a pe-
> riod of unusual prosperity, and it laid the foundation for Eng-
> land's emergence as a leading commercial power.

The two thoughts joined by *and* are clearly citing important facts about Queen Elizabeth's reign.

IMPROPER: The reign of Queen Elizabeth brought to England a period of unusual prosperity, and Shakespeare wrote many of his plays during her reign.

Two thoughts are cited, but the reason for the connection between these two thoughts is not clear. The reader may wonder whether the sentence is meant to emphasize one of two statements, but there is no indication which of the two statements is the more important.

IMPROVED: The reign of Queen Elizabeth brought to England a period of economic prosperity and cultural activity; Shakespeare, for instance, wrote many of his plays during her reign.

The relationship between the two thoughts is now clear. The emphasis is upon Elizabeth's reign; Shakespeare is merely an example.

IMPROPER: Shakespeare grew up during the reign of Queen Elizabeth, and his plays are among the greatest ever written.

The sentence gives no reason for joining these two ideas. They are merely strung together randomly.

IMPROVED: I remember very little from my studies in Shakespeare. I remember that he grew up during the reign of Queen Elizabeth and that his plays are among the greatest ever written.

The connection is a feeble one, but at least there is a connection.

---

13 L   If you use a coordinating conjunction, be sure that it expresses the relationship that you intend to express.

IMPROPER: War has been mankind's solution to problems since the beginning of history, and world leaders are now determined to resolve their differences through open discussion and compromise.

The two thoughts are being contrasted; hence, *and* is improper.

IMPROVED: War has been mankind's solution to problems since the beginning of history, *but* world leaders are now determined to resolve their differences through open discussion and compromise.

BETTER: Although war has been mankind's solution to problems since the beginning of history, world leaders are now determined to resolve their differences through open discussion and compromise.

Use *and* to express similarity; use *but* to express contrast.

14

Shifts

A shift is a change in pattern: writers may begin with one point of view but alter that point of view before they conclude. Carelessness and distraction often contribute to unnecessary shifts: writers may simply forget how they have begun. They forget that, having committed themselves to one point of view, they are obliged to continue with that point of view. Shifts are not necessarily wrong in the sense that the expression *They is coming* is wrong. Rather, unnecessary shifts impede the flow of the writing and often distract, perhaps even confuse, the reader. Furthermore, the reader may lose confidence in the writer: "If the writing is careless and inattentive to detail, perhaps the content is equally careless and inattentive to detail. Can I take seriously a writer who seems to have been distracted?"

14 A Avoid unnecessary shifts in the tense of verbs. If you are writing in the present tense, keep your main verbs in the present tense. If you are writing in the past tense, do not use the present tense. The following paragraph illustrates an unnecessary shift of tenses:

In the first act of the play, Dr. Stockmann *was living* a comfortable life, and the townspeople *had* a high regard for him. He *was* a successful doctor and an influential member of the community. But when he *discovers* that the town's public baths *are* polluted and *campaigns* to get the baths closed, the people *turn* against him.

In the first part of this paragraph, the writer uses the past tense: *was living . . . had . . . was.* But in the second half, the writer shifts unnecessarily into the present: *discovers . . . are . . . campaigns . . . turn.* The writer should have made all the earlier verbs present or all the later verbs past.

In the first act of the play, Dr. Stockmann *was living* a comfortable life, and the townspeople *had* a high regard for him. He *was* a successful doctor and an influential member of the community. But when he *discovered* that the town's public baths *were* polluted and *campaigned* to get the baths closed, the people *turned* against him.

---

14 B   Avoid unnecessary shifts between active and passive voice.

WEAK: Casey Jones managed to save the lives of his passengers, but his own life was lost when his train, the *Cannon Ball,* collided with another train.

There is no reason for the shift into the passive *his own life was lost;* in fact, it disrupts the sentence. The sentence should read:

Casey Jones managed to save the lives of his passengers but lost his own life when his train, the *Cannon Ball,* collided with another train.

---

14 C   Avoid shifts in number.

WEAK: *A citizen* should take an interest in local government. If *they* don't, *they* may find *themselves* faced with irresponsible leaders.

In this sentence, the *they* is plural while its antecedent *citizen* is singular. The shift can be easily corrected by making the antecedent plural:

Citizens should take an interest in local government. If *they* don't, *they* may find *themselves* faced with irresponsible leaders.

14 D   Avoid shifts in person. (See also Section 4 F.)

> WEAK: *Citizens* should take an interest in local government. If *you* don't, *you* may find *yourself* faced with irresponsible leaders.

Here, the pronouns *(you, yourself)* are in the second person while the antecedent *(citizens)* is in the third person. There are two ways to correct this sentence: use a consistent second person:

> *You* should take an interest in local government. If *you* don't, *you* may find *yourself* faced with irresponsible leaders.

or a consistent third person:

> *Citizens* should take an interest in local government. If *they* don't, *they* may find *themselves* faced with irresponsible leaders.

14 E   Avoid unnecessary shifts in mood.

Note how the following passages mixes indicatives with subjunctives with imperatives:

> A person who wants to read more efficiently *should train* himself in a few simple habits. First of all, *he should* skim the chapter. While he skims the chapter, *he looks* for the major subheads and thereby *gets* an idea of how the chapter is structured. Then *it is time to read* the whole chapter more carefully. In this reading, *take* brief notes and *try* to summarize to yourself what you have read.

All the verbs should be of the same mood:

a) They can all be in the conditional:

> A person . . . should train . . . he should skim . . . he should look . . . and thereby get. . . . Then he should read . . . he should take . . . and try to summarize to himself what he has read.

b) They can all be in the indicative:

> A person . . . trains himself . . . he skims . . . he looks . . . and thereby gets. . . . Then he reads . . . he takes brief notes and tries to summarize to himself what he has read.

c) They can all be in the imperative:

If you want to read more efficiently, train yourself . . . skim the chapter. While skimming, look . . . and thereby get. . . . Then read . . . take brief notes and try to summarize to yourself what you have read.

d) They can all be introduced by *let:*

If a person wants to read more efficiently, let him train . . . let him skim . . . let him look . . . and thereby get. . . . Then let him read . . . let him take brief notes and try to summarize to himself what he has read.

---

14 F Avoid unnecessary shifts in sentence structure — that is, shifts in parallelism, balance, or grammatical construction.

> WEAK: The treaty has three goals: to improve trade relationships, to lessen ideological misunderstanding, and the fostering of cultural exchanges.

The faulty parallelism here (see Sections 13 A and 13 B) joins *to improve* and *to lessen* with *fostering. Fostering* should be changed to an infinitive:

The treaty has three goals: to improve trade relationships, to lessen ideological misunderstandings, and to foster cultural exchanges.

> WEAK: Writers have warned us not to be complacent and that we should not elect complacent leaders.

Not to be and *that we should not elect* are not the same grammatical structure. The sentence should be rewritten:

Writers have warned us *not to be* complacent and *not to elect* complacent leaders.

The following sentence illustrates an even more obvious shift in construction:

Herb and Sam were talking during their spelling lesson what a beautiful day it was and how it was a perfect day for fishing.

This sentence may be fine in a totally informal and colloquial context. But it is a good example of how a sentence tries to combine two different types of constructions:

Herb and Sam were talking (about)
- what a beautiful day it was
- *and*
- how it was a perfect day for fishing.

The sentence can be improved.

Herb and Sam were talking during their spelling lesson. "What a beautiful day it is," they agreed, "and what a perfect day for fishing."

or

Herb and Sam were talking during their spelling lesson about what a beautiful day it was — a perfect one for fishing.

---

14 G   Avoid unnecessary shifts in the level of diction.

By level of diction is meant the type of language that you are using. If you are using formal English, avoid colloquial expressions, clichés, and other informalities.

At this point in the battle, there was no doubt that the British were being worsted; in fact, after a series of raids, the British had not only lost considerable ground but had also suffered serious losses. Therefore, Major Lartner's sudden idea did not seem as screwy to General Warthelwaithe as it does now to historians. Since Warthelwaithe was a person who had about as much stability as a feather in a windstorm — in fact, many who knew him felt that he was a bit off his rocker — and since he was a person who would often rush in where wise men fear to tread, it is not surprising that he would greet a plan such as Lartner's with enthusiasm, for Lartner's plan called for bold and unorthodox action, qualities that instantly appealed to the general.

The writing here is clearly quite elevated, the tone is serious, and the sentence structure fairly sophisticated — this is indeed formal writing. But note that certain words and phrases seem out of place:

a) *screwy*. This is much too informal a word for this context. Perhaps *impractical* or even *foolish* might be substituted.

b) *who had about as much stability as a feather in a windstorm.*

This may be an attempt at vividness, but it's a feeble and an inappropriate attempt; furthermore, it's wordy. Perhaps *who was unstable* might be substituted.

c) *a bit off his rocker.* This expression is far too colloquial; furthermore, it has been used so often that it has become a cliché. Perhaps *slightly mad* might be substituted.

d) *a person who would often rush in where wise men fear to tread.* This expression smacks of cliché and is also wordy. Perhaps *a reckless person* might be substituted.

Possible revision:

Therefore, Major Lartner's sudden idea did not seem as foolish to General Warthelwaithe as it does now to historians. Since Warthelwaithe was both an unstable and a reckless person — in fact, many who knew him felt that he was a bit mad — it is not surprising that . . . .

15

Structuring Sentences and Paragraphs

Inexperienced writers sometimes tend to write a series of simple sentences:

The War of 1812 was between America and England. The British had stirred up Indians. They had captured many American seamen. This act was called *impressment*. President Monroe declared war on June 18, 1812. Neither side had a decisive military victory. The British burned many buildings in Washington. The war ended in 1814. The peace treaty was signed on December 24. It was called the Treaty of Ghent.

Such writing presents information but it does so indiscriminately. No attempt is made to show any relationship among the various ideas or to present those ideas in a logical order. Because of the string of similar sounding sentences, there is a choppiness to the writing.

Experienced writers, on the other hand, try to vary the types of sentences that they use; they try to express relationships among the ideas that they are presenting and they try to present those ideas with fluency:

Because the British had been inciting the Indians and had been capturing, or *impressing* American seamen, President Monroe declared war on June 18, 1812. Although the British did burn many buildings in Washington, neither side had a decisive military victory, and the War of 1812 ended on December 24, 1814, with the signing of the Treaty of Ghent.

There are five techniques that can aid writers in structuring their sentences: coordination, subordination, transition, unity, and coherence. These techniques will contribute to clarity and to smoothness; they will allow a writer to distinguish a main idea from a supporting idea; they will assist a writer in presenting ideas in a logical and organized fashion; and they will help the reader in determining the relationship between one thought and another.

COORDINATION AND SUBORDINATION

The techniques of coordinating or subordinating ideas allow us to suggest the relative importance of those ideas. Coordination, a topic already mentioned in Chapter 13, is the process by which ideas equal in importance are joined. Subordination, on the other hand, is the process of structuring sentences in such a way that a main idea receives more emphasis than the less important ideas.

INDEPENDENT THOUGHTS: Leonard Bernstein wrote both *Candide* and *West Side Story. Candide* has more tuneful melodies than *West Side Story. West Side Story* is more popular.

COORDINATED THOUGHTS: Leonard Bernstein's *Candide* has more tuneful melodies than his *West Side Story,* but it is not as popular.

SUBORDINATED THOUGHTS: Although Leonard Bernstein's *Candide* has more tuneful melodies than his *West Side Story,* it is not as popular.

The first example is choppy and immature. The second and third are more compactly and more forcefully written.

A writer frequently has to choose between coordination and subordination. Coordination should be used when the equality of the thoughts is important; subordination should be used when one thought is more important than the other thought or thoughts of the sentence.

Coordination is achieved through coordinate conjunctions: *and, but, or, nor, for.*

Subordination is achieved through subordinate conjunctions: *when, since, although, because, after, as, as soon as, whenever, if, even though, while, in order to, so that.* These conjunctions express a relationship such as cause *(because, since),* condition *(if, unless),* concession *(even though, although),* purpose *(that, in order that, lest),* time *(when, as, after, as soon as, while, before, until),* place *(wherever, everywhere),* and result *(so . . . that).* Subordination can also be achieved through a relative pronoun: *who/whose/whom, which, that.*

When deciding how to structure a sentence, first itemize, either in your mind or on paper, the data. For instance:

(1) Rasputin was a monk   (2) lived in Russia   (3) had enormous influence over the emperor   (4) had unusual personal charm   (5) was considered holy   (6) people thought he was mysterious   (7) many people suspected that he was actually the one ruling Russia   (8) was assassinated in 1916

Then determine the main point(s) of those data. If there is one main point, the data should be built around it. If there is more than one main point, there should be either two separate sentences or a single sentence coordinating those main points. In the example above, points (3) and (7) seem to be the most important; since (7) seems to be the result of (3), we can now write the main idea:

Rasputin had such enormous influence over the emperor that many people suspected that he was the one who was actually ruling Russia.

Then, we see if there is any relationship among the remaining data. Items (4), (5), and (6) all deal with Rasputin's personal attributes; hence they can be coordinated and connected with the reason for his having such enormous influence. Statement (2) can be incorporated with statement (7) since both establish the location as being Russia. Statement (1) seems more descriptive than essential and can therefore be relegated to a subordinate position. Finally, statement (8), since it seems out of place with the rest of the data, can be made a separate unit of thought:

The monk Rasputin, because of his unusual personal charm and his air of both sanctity and mystery, gained such a position of influence over the emperor that many people suspected that it was he who was actually ruling Russia. He was ultimately assassinated in 1916.

Suppose that the final piece of information is the crucial one. If we know that Rasputin was assassinated because some people felt that he was too powerful, then we can recast the sentence:

Rasputin was a monk characterized by unusual personal charm and by an air of both sanctity and mystery, qualities that gained him a position of enormous influence over the emperor; however, when it was suspected that it was he who was actually ruling Russia, he was assassinated in 1916.

The relationship among the thoughts is clear; it is a cause and effect relationship: Rasputin's personal qualities led to his influence over the emperor and that influence led to his assassination.

When joining thoughts, be careful of the following:

a) Do not try to coordinate thoughts of unequal value.

WEAK: Commodore Perry reached Japan in 1853, and his entry was the beginning of western influence in Japan.

IMPROVED: Commodore Perry's entry into Japan in 1853 was the beginning of western influence in Japan.

Pay particular attention not to abuse the word *and*. Do not join thoughts with *and* when those thoughts should more properly express some other relationship to one other—that is, do not be guilty of **improper coordination:**

WEAK: Commodore Perry opened up Japan in 1853, and soon after that there was commerce between Japan and the United States.

IMPROVED: Commerce began between Japan and the United States soon after Commodore Perry opened up Japan in 1853.

b) If one thought is more important than the other thoughts of a sentence, place the important thought in the main clause and subordinate the less important thoughts.

When Commodore Perry entered Japan in 1853, the beginning of western influence entered with him.

A writer will sometimes carelessly reverse the important and the less important ideas. This is called **faulty subordination:**

WEAK: Although Commodore Perry had enormous influence both upon the American navy and upon the trade relationship between the United States and Japan, his early career was undistinguished.

The emphasis of the ideas should be reversed:

Although Commodore Perry's early career was undistinguished, he had enormous influence both upon the American navy and upon the trade relationship between the United States and Japan.

TRANSITION

Transition may occur from one sentence to another or from one paragraph to another or, for that matter, from one chapter to another. Transition is the technique by which the logical connection between two thoughts is indicated. Transition tells the reader how one thought connects with or is related to the thought that immediately precedes or follows. Transition can help to emphasize what the writer feels is important, and it can also help to keep an idea fresh in the reader's mind.

The following are some of the ways of expressing transition:

a) Repetition of a word or phrase:

The reasons for the many wars throughout history are as complex and manifold as they are damning to humans. *Wars* have been a constant blot upon the conscience of mankind.

b) Repetition of a related word or phrase:

The reasons for the many wars throughout history are as complex and manifold as they are damning to humans. *Man's need for aggression* has been a constant blot upon the conscience of the human race.

c) Connection by way of a demonstrative word:

The reasons for the many wars throughout history are as complex and manifold as they are damning to humans. *These explanations* often center upon political or economic or religious areas, but rarely do they cite the chief villain: man's need for aggression and man's need for violence.

d) Specific transitional words, such as:

still	*therefore*	*finally*
yet	*consequently*	*first*
however	*thus*	*second*
nevertheless	*hence*	*next*
on the other hand	*indeed*	*again*
after all	*in fact*	*to be sure*
on the contrary	*for instance*	*certainly*
similarly	*furthermore*	*meanwhile*
likewise	*moreover*	*then*
in the same way	*in addition*	*but*

e) The processes of coordination and subordination that were described earlier in this chapter.

The following passage has been written without any transition. Note how choppy it sounds and how ununified the thoughts seem to be.

The five offspring of Cronos and Rhea had no affection for their father; they wanted to get rid of him. They declared war. This war was the great Titanomachia. It lasted for ten years.

There was a Titan named Prometheus. He was extremely clever and resourceful. He had been told by his mother that it would be wit, not physical violence, that would settle the war. During this war he tried to give ideas to the Titans; they had no appreciation for the subtleties of his strategies; they expected that brute strength and force was all that was needed. Prometheus suggested that Cronos recall his brothers who had been banished to Hades and enlist the aid of these brothers. Cronos refused, perhaps out of native stupidity, perhaps out of pride; perhaps he was afraid.

Prometheus realized that Cronos had no sense and he went to Zeus. He offered the same advice. Zeus agreed. He freed the three Cyclops; they were so grateful that they each gave Zeus a gift to express their appreciation. They gave a gift to the other two males. Zeus freed the Hecatoncheires, those hundred-handed, fifty-headed aberrations born of the Earth and the Sky.

Now, reread the passage, this time with added transitional elements. Notice how much smoother the second passage is. It is much easier to see how one sentence relates to another.

The five offspring of Cronos and Rhea had no affection for their father *and, in fact,* they wanted to get rid of him. *Hence,* they declared war, the great Titanomachia, *a war that* lasted for ten years.

At this time there was a Titan named Prometheus, an extremely clever and resourceful being. He had been told by his mother that it would be wit, not physical violence, that would settle *this conflict; consequently,* during *this battle* he tried to give ideas to the Titans, *but* they had no appreciation for the subtleties of his strategies; *rather,* they expected that brute strength and force was all that was needed. Prometheus suggested, *for instance,* that Cronos recall his brothers who had been banished to Hades and enlist the aid of these *mighty beings. But* Cronos refused, perhaps out of native stupidity, perhaps out of pride, perhaps *out of fear.*

At any rate, realizing that Cronos had no sense, Prometheus went to Zeus *and* offered the same advice. He *first* freed the three Cyclops; they were so grateful that they each gave gifts to Zeus *and* to the other two males. *Next,* Zeus freed the Hecatoncheires, those hundred-handed, fifty-headed aberrations born of the Earth and the Sky.*

UNITY AND COHERENCE

Every paragraph is built upon one central idea. This central idea, sometimes called the topic sentence, forms the basis of the paragraph. Unity is the principle by which all the thoughts in a paragraph contribute to that central, controlling idea. A paragraph is said to be unified if all the thoughts do relate to that idea. If irrelevancies enter a paragraph, then that paragraph is said to lack unity.

*Adapted from Thomas H. Carpenter and Robert J. Gula, *Mythology: Greek and Roman* (Wellesley Hills, Mass.: Independent School Press), p. 5.

The same principle is true for an essay. An essay has a central, controlling idea—i.e., a thesis. If all the paragraphs contribute to that idea, the essay is said to be unified. If there are paragraphs that are irrelevant, then the essay is said to lack unity.

Coherence deals with the order in which the thoughts appear. A coherent paragraph is one in which the sentences move clearly and logically from one to the next. The reader has no trouble determining how a particular sentence relates to the previous sentence and how a particular sentence relates to the paragraph as a whole. Similarly, a coherent essay is one in which the paragraphs move clearly and logically from one to the next. The reader has no trouble in determining how a particular paragraph relates to the previous paragraph and how a particular paragraph relates to the essay as a whole.

Unity, therefore, deals with relevance. Coherence deals with logical order.

A paragraph that lacks unity or coherence will confuse readers. They will not be able to follow the train of thought; they will probably not be able to determine what the most important idea of the paragraph is; and because of this confusion they will probably become frustrated.

Let us examine a paragraph that lacks both unity and coherence:

Only when there is a compelling need should the government have the right to classify information and withhold it from the citizens—as when it concerns necessarily secret technical and tactical aspects of military planning and activity, or covert intelligence operations abroad, or confidential diplomacy. For the public has a fundamental right, under the Constitution, to know what its government is up to. It follows that the government had no right to conceal from the American people the fact that it was bombing Cambodia, with no legislative or constitutional justification at all—since this was not news to the Cambodians or their allies. It is a further consequence of the public's fundamental right that all classification should be for a short and fixed period of time, and, moreover, that it should be done by a quasi-judicial commission, independent of the government—

especially since, as we know, it is the habit of administrations, when they are highly secretive, to protect themselves by keeping the public ignorant of their mistakes and their unwarranted acts.*

First of all, the paragraph has a variety of concerns: that the government should not classify information except under extreme circumstances — a general statement; that the government should not have concealed the fact that it was bombing Cambodia — a specific criticism; that a body other than the government should determine what information should be classified — a specific recommendation; that all classification should be for a limited period of time — another specific recommendation.

Now, what is the point of the paragraph? Is it a criticism of the government's attempt to conceal the fact that Cambodia was being bombed? Is it a criticism of the government's policy toward classification in general? Or is it a recommendation concerning the process of classification?

The paragraph tries to do too much and in the process it loses sight of any clear point: it doesn't know what it is doing or what point it is making. In short, it lacks unity.

There are still other weaknesses. Examine, for instance, the following:

It follows that the government had no right to conceal from the American people the fact that it was bombing Cambodia, with no legislative or constitutional justification at all — since this was not news to the Cambodians or their allies.

What is the relationship among these ideas? Does the writer mean to say:

It is permissible for the government to withhold secret aspects of military planning. But, since the Cambodians knew about the bombing, it was not a secret. Therefore, it was not permissible for the government to withhold the fact that it was bombing Cambodia.

*From Monroe C. Beardsley, *Thinking Straight,* 4th ed. (Englewood Cliffs, N.J.: Prentice-Hall, 1975), p. 30.

A careful reading of the original paragraph suggests that this cannot be the intention of the writer. The paragraph, after all, uses the words "with no legislative or constitutional justification." Perhaps, therefore, what the writer means is:

It is permissible for the government to bomb other countries as long as it has legislative or constitutional justification. There was no legislative or constitutional justification in the bombing of Cambodia. Therefore, the bombing of Cambodia was unjustifiable.

Again, because of the lack of coherence, it is difficult to determine just what the writer is trying to say.

Notice that the phrase "all classification should be for a short and fixed period of time" has no specific connection with the rest of the paragraph. The writer has again forced the reader—if the reader is patient enough—to make an inference and to speculate whether the writer actually means:

Since it is the habit of administrators, when they are highly secretive, to protect themselves by keeping the public ignorant of their mistakes and their unwarranted acts, all classification should be done by a quasi-judicial commission, independent of the government, and this classification should be for a short and fixed period of time.

The fact that the ideas do not follow each other logically —i.e., the absence of coherence—frustrates the reader. The reader is invited to speculate, and speculations all too easily lead to faulty inferences and misinterpretation. It is the responsibility of writers to say what they mean to say and to express themselves clearly enough so that their words will not invite misrepresentation. Writers must not ask their reader to do their work for them, and writers should never find themselves in the position of making the disclaimer, "What I meant to say was . . ."

The following points will summarize most of the discussion of this chapter.

15 A   A paragraph should have one and only one basic, controlling idea — the topic sentence.

15 B   That basic idea should be obvious and clear.

15 C   All the other thoughts of the paragraph should contribute to and be related to that basic idea.

15 D   The main idea of a sentence should be clearly differentiated from the supporting or less important ideas.

15 E   The thoughts should proceed logically from one to the next.

15 F   The writing should help the reader to ascertain that logical connection.

To these points may be added the following recommendations concerning the manner in which you build your sentences.

15 G   Vary your sentence structure. Aim for variety both in the length of the sentences and in the types of sentences that you use. Try to avoid a series of similar sounding sen-

tences, for sentences that sound alike soon become monotonous. Observe the monotony of the following paragraph:

Odysseus had a great number of difficulties in returning home to Ithaca. After he left Troy, he was shipwrecked and had to swim for his life. When he got to land, he was nurtured by Calypso and spent several years with her. After he became restless, he prevailed upon her to let him go and she complied. Soon after he left her, he was overcome by another storm and almost lost his life. When he survived this storm, he found himself in the land of the Phaeacians and he spent a short time there. While he was in Phaeacia, he heard stories about the Trojan War and, as he was reminded of his lost companions, he wept.

Notice the repetitious pattern and the number of similar sounding sentences: subordinate clause – subject – verb – complement – *and* – (subject –) verb (– complement). Varying the sentence structure would have strengthened this paragraph:

Odysseus had a great number of difficulties in returning home to Ithaca. After he left Troy, he was shipwrecked twice and almost lost his life on each occasion. He was first nurtured by Calypso but, when after several years he became restless, he prevailed upon her to let him leave. The second storm cast him upon the land of the Phaeacians. He spent only a short time there. Minstrels would often sing of the Trojan War, and as he heard their stories, he wept at the memory of his lost companions.

---

15 H   Don't overload your sentences. Don't write sentences that are asked to support more than a sentence can support.

When Odysseus arrived on Calypso's island, he was close to death, and the goddess, who nurtured him and restored him to health, eventually fell in love with him and tried to keep him with her against his will, but Odysseus was too eager to return home and see his wife, whom he had not seen in almost two decades, and so he prevailed upon Calypso to let him leave.

There are simply too many thoughts in this sentence.

The various thoughts should be separated and simplified:

When Odysseus arrived on Calypso's island, he was close to death. Nurturing him, the goddess restored him to health; however, she also fell in love with him. She tried to keep him with her against his will, but Odysseus was eager to return home. Not having seen his wife in almost two decades, he was anxious to be reunited with her. Therefore, he prevailed upon Calypso to let him leave.

---

15 I   Don't use language that is unnecessarily complex.

The proposed program will self-consciously seek to educate in both' aspects of intellectual endeavor: disciplined and discrete utilization of specific analytic disciplines and imaginative holistic endeavors at synthetic comprehension.

The sentence here should express more naturally just what it means.

There are two different approaches toward education. The first concerns specific academic subjects The second concerns the relationships among those subjects. The proposed program will try to incorporate both approaches.

---

15 J   Similarly, don't use unnecessary words.

Despite the fact that the matters under consideration are of a confidential nature, there is no reason for us to feel under any restrictions in conducting discussions among ourselves in the privacy of our own chambers.

This sentence should be edited:

Although these matters are confidential, we can still discuss them privately among ourselves.

punctuation and mechanics

Punctuation: A Quick Overview

Punctuation mark	Its name	Main use	Examples	Discussed in chapter
.	period	indicates the end of a statement	We are coming. We wondered who was coming.	16
		indicates the end of an abbreviation	Dr.	30
;	semicolon	equivalent to a weak period; separates two closely related sentences	My son gave a recital last week; he is a fine musician.	16
?	question mark	indicates a question	Who is coming?	21
!	exclamation point	indicates a strong or an emotional utterance	Get out of here! Damn!	21
,	comma	i) separates two sentences joined by a conjunction	I will leave you, but I will do so reluctantly.	16
		ii) indicates an interrupting element	Mr. Smith, my uncle, was in an accident.	17 & 18
			Mr. Smith, since he was driving too fast, was in an accident.	
		iii) separates elements in a series	I went to Paris, Rome, and Bombay.	18
" "	quotation marks	indicates someone else's words	The Declaration of Independence says "that all men are created equal."	19
:	colon	indicates that an explanation or a series is to follow	I wouldn't trust him: he's a liar.	20

Punctuation mark	Its name	Main use	Examples	Discussed in chapter
—	dash	indicates a side-thought or an afterthought or a piece of extraneous information	John Adams—he must be distinguished from John Quincy Adams—assumed office in 1825.	22
( )	parentheses	similar to a dash but more formal; contains additional but nonessential information	George Herman ("Babe") Ruth is one of our great American heroes.	23
[ ]	brackets	used inside a quotation to indicate words other than by the source being quoted	The Declaration of Independence says "that all men [men is used in the generic sense referring to human beings in general] are created equal."	24
. . .	ellipsis	indicates that words have been omitted from a quotation	The Declaration of Independence says "that all men . . . are endowed . . . with certain unalienable rights."	25
-	hyphen	divides a word between one line and the next	compo-sition	26
		joins two words that are thought of as one	self-contained long-awaited action	
'	apostrophe	indicates that a letter has been omitted	wasn't	28
		indicates possession	Sarah's	
_____	underline	indicates italics	the Queen Mary	27

16

First Principles of Punctuation: Simple and Compound Sentences

16 A   A single complete thought — that is, a single sentence or single independent clause — must end with either a period, semicolon, exclamation point, or question mark.

16 B   When you have two complete thoughts — that is, two sentences — without any conjunction between those two complete thoughts, the two thoughts must be separated by either a period or a semicolon.

Zeus was the head of the Greek gods. His palace was on Mt. Olympus.

16 C   A semicolon substitutes for the period when there is a close connection between the complete thoughts.

Zeus was the god of the skies; he controlled the weather.

16 D   If there is no punctuation between two complete thoughts, the error is known as a **run-on sentence.** This is one of the three most serious punctuation errors.

Zeus was the head of the Greek gods↓his wife was Hera.

The error should be corrected by separating the two sentences with a period or semicolon:

Zeus was the head of the Greek gods;↓his wife was Hera.

or

Zeus was the head of the Greek gods.↓His wife was Hera.

---

16 E If a comma instead of a period or semicolon separates two complete thoughts, the error is known as a **comma splice.** This is the second of the three most serious punctuation errors.

Hera was the queen of the Greek gods,↓she was the equivalent of Juno in Roman mythology.

The error can easily be corrected by changing the comma to a period or semicolon:

Hera was the queen of the Greek gods;↓she was the equivalent of Juno in Roman mythology.

or

Hera was the queen of the Greek gods.↓She was the equivalent of Juno in Roman mythology.

---

16 F Make sure that each sentence is a complete thought — that it is a complete grammatical unit containing a subject and a verb. An incomplete sentence — a sentence that does not have either a subject or a finite verb — is called a **sentence fragment.** This is the third of the three most serious punctuation errors.

INCORRECT: Although exhausted, Dr. Schott persevered. Hoping that she would be able to identify the virus.

Hoping is not a complete verb; it is merely a verb form.

Hoping that she would be able to identify the virus is therefore a sentence fragment.

CORRECT: Although exhausted, Dr. Schott persevered,ˢ hoping that she would be able to identify the virus.

or

Although exhausted, Dr. Schott persevered. *She hoped* that she would be able to identify the virus.

INCORRECT: Our organization allows votes to be registered by proxy. Which is the process by which one person casts a vote in behalf of another person.

Which is the process is an incomplete thought; the second group of words is therefore a sentence fragment.

CORRECT: Our organization allows votes to be registered by proxy,ˢ which is the process by which one person casts a vote in behalf of another person.

or

Our organization allows votes to be registered by proxy. *This is* the process by which one person casts a vote in behalf of another person.

INCORRECT: Senator Joseph McCarthy seemed to have only one motivation. To find and expose Communists in every corner of the country.

To find and expose is an infinitive, not a complete verb; it introduces a sentence fragment.

CORRECT: Senator Joseph McCarthy seemed to have only one motivation,ˢ to find and expose Communists in every corner of the country.

Note: In almost all cases, the sentence fragment can be corrected by changing the period before the fragment to a comma.

---

16 G   If there are two or more complete thoughts connected by *and, or, for, nor,* or *but,* a comma separates each of the sentences.

I did not know the answer, but I knew I could find it in the encyclopedia.

I will always respect anyone who can play Liszt's music, for I realize that it is among the most difficult music ever written for the piano.

---

16 H When words like the following introduce a complete sentence, put a semicolon in front of them and a comma after them:

therefore	on the other hand	in fact	still
indeed	furthermore	moreover	yet
nevertheless	nonetheless	however	hence
consequently	for instance		

I tried as hard as I could; in fact, I could not have tried harder; nonetheless, I did not succeed; however, I have not yet given up hope; indeed, I shall continue to try.

---

16 I The words listed in Section 16 H above and the words *and, but,* and *nor* can sometimes begin a sentence when strong contrast is desired.

There are times when we must expect consistency. However, there are other times when a reliance upon consistency indicates a closed mind.

I investigated the matter as thoroughly as I could, and I was still confused. But there was one thing I was sure of: Mr. Stone had exceeded his authority.

Two common errors

---

16 J While *and, or, for, but,* and *nor* are preceded by a comma when these words separate two complete thoughts, a comma should not be used if the second thought is incomplete.

INCORRECT: I visited Paris, and Rome.

INCORRECT: Peter worked all night, but was unable to finish the report.

INCORRECT: You must either control your temper, or swallow your pride.

INCORRECT: I hope that everyone will arrive on time, and that we can start the meeting on schedule.

The comma should be deleted in each of these examples because the thought that follows the comma is not a complete one—that is, it is not a complete sentence. The only way the comma would be justified would be if the material that follows it formed a complete sentence:

I visited Paris, and *I spent* some time in Rome.

Peter worked all night, but *he was* unable to finish the report.

Either you must control your temper, or *you must swallow* your pride.

---

16 K   Never allow just one comma to stand between a subject and its verb or between a verb and its complement.

INCORRECT: The message of the manager and the cutbacks that
followed, indicated a decline in the company's stability.

INCORRECT: All the encouragement in the world, and even the best trainers in the world aren't going to make me a graceful dancer.

INCORRECT: It was apparent that I would have to tell the police, of the incident that I had just witnessed.

INCORRECT: It was apparent that I would have to tell the police, and my parents of the incident that I had witnessed.

In each of these sentences, the comma should be deleted. It serves no purpose; in fact, it needlessly fragments the sentence.

17

Punctuation of Phrases and Clauses

ADJECTIVAL AND ADVERBIAL EXPRESSIONS

An adjective phrase or clause is a group of words that adds descriptive information to another word or to other words. It is introduced by a participle or by a relative pronoun.

Documents *written in haste* often contain ambiguities.
Documents *that are written in haste* often contain ambiguities.

In each of these two examples, the italicized words add descriptive information. The words specify what type of documents are being referred to—that is, hastily written documents.

An adverbial phrase or clause is a group of words that begins with words such as the following:

when	since	after	as
because	whenever	although	if
as soon as	(in order) to	while	so that
(in order) that	before	lest	unless
even though			

Rather than adding descriptive information, adverbial expressions indicate a relationship to the rest of the sentence, such as that of time, cause, extent, concession, result, condition, or purpose.

The only difference between a phrase and a clause is

this: a clause contains a complete verb form; a phrase does not contain a complete verb form.

CLAUSE: *When we heard the shouts,* we knew we had better take shelter.

PHRASE: *Hearing the shouts,* we knew that we had better take shelter.

The shouts having been heard, we knew that we had better take shelter.

CLAUSE: The man *who is approaching us* is Senator Bereday.

PHRASE: The man *approaching us* is Senator Bereday.

However, for purposes of punctuation, it is not necessary to distinguish between a phrase and a clause.

---

17 A   Adverbial and adjectival expressions end with a comma when they come at the beginning of a sentence.

After Loki had caused the death of Baldur the Beautiful, he withdrew from Asgard and went into seclusion.

After causing the death of Baldur the Beautiful, Loki withdrew from Asgard and went into seclusion.

While planning the death of Baldur the Beautiful, Loki realized that he would never again be welcome among the Aesir.

To show his contempt for his fellow gods, Loki arranged for the death of Baldur the Beautiful.

Odin being outraged at the death of Baldur, he vowed vengence upon Loki.

Jealous of the attention that Baldur was constantly getting, Loki decided to plan his death.

---

17 B   Adverbial phrases or clauses are set off by commas when they appear in the middle of a sentence.

Loki, after he had caused the death of Baldur the Beautiful, withdrew from Asgard and went into seclusion.

The gods realized that, if they allowed Loki to remain at large, there would only be further trouble.

Loki, to show his contempt for his fellow gods, caused the death of Baldur the Beautiful.

17 C   If the adverbial expression comes at the end of a sentence, it is not usually preceded by a comma.

no comma
↓

Loki withdrew from Asgard and went into seclusion after he had caused the death of Baldur the Beautiful.

no comma
↓

The gods realized that there would be only further trouble if they allowed Loki to remain at large.

no comma
↓

Loki caused the death of Baldur the Beautiful to show his contempt for his fellow gods.

---

17 D   When an adjectival expression appears either within a sentence or at the end of a sentence, it is set off by commas only if it is not essential to the meaning of the sentence. In other words, if the expression could be omitted without distorting the meaning of the sentence, that phrase or clause should be set off by commas.

The Bill of Rights, not originally included in the Constitution, has become the basis of our personal liberties.

The words set off by commas could have been omitted without altering the meaning of the sentence. These words add descriptive information but not essential information.

The automobile, which has become an indispensable part of our society, sometimes seems as much a nuisance as a blessing.

Again, the words within the commas add only descriptive information. The sentence would not change its meaning if those words were omitted.

I have just been reading about Lord Byron, whose life I find enviably fascinating.

The words after the comma are not essential to the sentence. They merely add additional information.

Odin, becoming convinced that Loki had betrayed him and the other gods in Asgard, decided that the time had come to punish this traitor.

The words within the commas add important information but not essential information. The sentence would not have been altered if these words had been omitted.

---

17 E On the other hand, if an adjectival expression is essential to the meaning of a sentence — that is, if the omission of the expression would change the meaning of the sentence — then that expression must not be set off by commas.

Automobiles *that pollute the air* should be banned from the roads.

The italicized words are absolutely essential to the meaning of the sentence. Without those words, the sentence would say:

Automobiles should be banned from the roads.

a statement that distorts the meaning of the original sentence.

You should simply ignore people *who insult you.*

Again, the italicized expression is essential. Without it, the sentence would mean something entirely different:

You should simply ignore people.

The following is another example:

The Romans made a concerted effort to discover and exterminate all people *believing in Christianity.*

If one were to put a comma after *people,* the sentence would say that the Romans wanted to exterminate all people.

People *believing in Christianity* found their faith severely tested when the Romans conducted a campaign of religious persecution.

The italicized words are needed if the sentence is going to say what it wants to say.

17 F   Sometimes you have a choice as to whether or not to set off an adjectival expression with commas. If you do decide to set off the expression, make sure that there is a comma both in front of and after that expression.

INCORRECT: The plan, designed by the manager is a good one.
INCORRECT: The plan designed by the manager, is a good one.
CORRECT: The plan, designed by the manager, is a good one.
CORRECT: The plan designed by the manager is a good one.

Remember: you cannot have just one comma between the subject and its verb (Section 16 K).

APPOSITIVES

An appositive is a word or a group of words that identifies or renames a noun or a pronoun.

17 G   The appositive is set off by commas when it merely adds additional but unessential information.

The next day, *the twenty-third of June,* we left for Brussels.

James Monroe, *the nation's fifth President,* made it clear that America would tolerate no foreign intervention in her matters. This policy, *the Monroe Doctrine,* had significant influence upon the political relationship between Europe and the United States, *an influence that contributed to the U.S.'s involvement in World War I.*

17 H   The appositive is not set off by commas when it adds essential information to the sentence.

I approve much more of Nixon *the diplomat* than of Nixon *the politician.*

PREPOSITIONAL PHRASES

17 I A prepositional phrase is usually not set off by commas.

The Senate with its usual caution decided to amend the bill submitted by the President concerning the terms of the Panama Canal.

17 J However, sometimes the comma is needed after an introductory phrase to avoid misreading or misinterpretation.

For her, effort was more important than performance.

For her effort, she was rewarded.

NOUN CLAUSES

A noun clause is a group of words with a subject and verb that acts in the same way a noun can act, especially as a subject and as an object of a sentence.

17 K Noun clauses are not set off by commas.

No one knew *who had sent the letter.*

We all believed *that the decision was a good one.*

I will ask *how he plans to do it.*

That the earth is just a speck becomes more and more apparent as we begin to appreciate the vastness of the universe.

What you do and what you say are sometimes at odds.

Why the Senate decided to veto the bill is a mystery to me.

The Comma: Important Uses

1. *To separate complete thoughts joined by* and, or, nor, for, but: (16 G)

   I was perplexed by the speech, for it seemed confusing.

2. *After introductory elements:*   (17 A)

   Because you have arrived late, you will have to stand.

3. *To separate interrupting elements within a sentence:*
   a) PHRASES AND CLAUSES: The judge, after hearing the evidence, made his decision quickly.   (17 B)
   b) APPOSITIVES: Mr. Patey, the assistant treasurer, will submit his report tomorrow.   (17 G)
   c) DIRECT ADDRESS: I warned you, Pat, that the movie was boring.   (18 E)
   d) INTERJECTIONS, WORDS OF EMPHASIS AND CONTRAST, PAREN-THETICAL EXPRESSIONS: The noise, I think, came from the cellar.   (18 E)
   e) DATES AND PLACES: She was born on September 16, 1832, in Roanoke, Virginia, on a small plantation.   (18 E)

4. *In a series:*   (18 A)

   You should gather the data, study it, and evaluate it.

5. *After certain transitional words:*   (16 H)

   The senator was embarrassed; in fact, he was so upset that he could not continue speaking.

6. *After certain abbreviations:*   (18 F)

   Several countries—e.g., Iran and Saudi Arabia—are determined to ignore all Western influences.

7. *To separate independent adjectives:*   (18 G)

   The loud, monotonous noise began to irritate me.

8. *In quotations:*   (19 C, D, F)

   "I will not argue," replied the witness, "but I still disagree."

The Comma: Common Errors

1. *The comma splice:* (16 E)

   wrong
   ↓

   I didn't finish the book, it was too long.

2. *Between **two** parallel words or phrases:* (16 J, 18 B)

   delete
   ↓

   The treasurer's report, and his proposals were acceptable
   to the committee.

3. *Between subject and verb or between verb and complement:* (16 K)

   delete
   ↓

   I hesitated to tell her, just what was on my mind.

4. *Before an essential phrase or clause at the end of a sentence:* (17 C)

   delete
   ↓

   We were embarrassed, when we discovered our error.

5. *Around essential words within a sentence:* (17 E)

   delete   delete
   ↓   ↓

   People, who constantly commit crimes, should be imprisoned.

6. *Omission of a comma in an interruption:* (17 F)
   The members of Congress, as well as the members of the Presi-

   comma needed
   ↓

   dent's cabinet were outraged at what they heard.

7. *With noun clauses:* (17 K)

   delete
   ↓

   What I heard from Greg, does not agree with what you told me.

8. ***After** the last item in a series:* (18 C)
   I read novels by Sinclair Lewis, William Faulkner, and Ayn

   delete
   ↓

   Rand, during my seminar in American literature.

9. *Before a zip code:* (18 E)

   delete
   ↓

   Newark, New Jersey, 07103

10. *To separate dependent adjectives:* (18 H)

    delete
    ↓

    Ancient, wall paintings were discovered in Arizona.

11. *Before an indirect quotation:* (19 P)

    delete
    ↓

    The Bill of Rights says, that all people are equal in the eyes of the law.

18

The Comma:
Miscellaneous Uses

IN SERIES

18 A   Use commas to separate three or more items in a series.

Note: Some writers omit the comma before the *and*. This is an acceptable practice only if there is no risk of confusing the reader.

optional
↓
My favorite novelists are Dickens, Thackeray, and Hardy.

I hope that you will attend the lecture, listen carefully, take
optional
↓
good notes, and give me a summary when you return.

I do not envy people in public service. They have little privacy,

required
↓
the press constantly badgers them, and their families rarely see them.

The second comma in the third example is needed. Without it a reader might join *families* with *them: the press constantly badgers them and their families*. In the first two examples, however, the comma before the *and* could be removed without causing ambiguity.

18 B   Do not use a comma between just two items.

no comma
↓
My favorite novelists are Dickens and Hardy.

18 C   Do not use a comma after the last item of a series.

no comma
↓
Freia was an attractive, winsome, and charming goddess.

no comma
↓
You will need sodium, chlorine, and water to complete this experiment.

18 D   Semicolons can replace commas when there are other commas already being used to separate items in a series. The semicolon here merely prevents a congestion of commas.

Only three senators were absent from the meeting: Senator
↓
Palmer, who was out of the country; Senator Curtis, who had
↓
made a prior commitment; and Senator Bullard, who was delivering a commencement address.

↓   ↓
I visited Springfield, Illinois; Middletown, Connecticut; and Portland, Oregon.

INTERRUPTIONS

18 E   Commas separate words that interrupt a sentence, such as

a) **words in direct address:**

I warned you, David, not to try to fix the clock.

Be quiet, you simple-minded ninny, and pay attention.

b) appositives:

The First World War, that war to end all wars, was only the prelude.

c) interjections and parenthetical expressions:

Well, I hope you realize that you have just ruined the project.

You realize, { naturally, / of course, / I suspect, / don't you, / after all, } that you have just ruined the project.

I'm afraid, alas, that I have made a serious error.

d) words of contrast, emphasis, and qualification:

I think, { in fact, / furthermore, / on the other hand, / nevertheless, / however, } that the matter should be investigated.

e) the second and all additional elements of an address:

I will always remember Lincoln, Nebraska, with great fondness.

Please forward the letter to Professor and Mrs. Harwood, 128 Drury Lane, Melrose, Massachusetts 02176, and you should get a quick response.

Note: there is no comma between a state and its zip code.

f) in dates:

When a year is part of a date, there is a comma after it. When a year is joined with a month and a date, there is a comma both before and after it. When a year appears with just a month, the comma before the year is optional.

September 2, 1945, was the official end of World War II.

optional

In December, 1941, an event occurred that altered the course of history.

MISCELLANEOUS

18 F   Both a period and a comma are used after the abbreviations *etc., e.g.,* and *i.e.,* when the sentence continues after the abbreviation.

Several parts of speech — e.g., the pronoun and the verb — are often misused.

Those presidents — i.e., Nixon and Harding — had administrations noted for corruption.

I enjoy baseball, basketball, soccer, etc., but am not skilled at any of these sports.

18 G   A comma should separate independent adjectives that are not joined by a conjunction. (Adjectives are independent when they can be reversed.)

I have a magnificent, dynamic recording of Stravinsky's *The Rite of Spring*.

These adjectives could just as easily have been reversed:

I have a dynamic, magnificent recording of Stravinsky's *The Rite of Spring*.

18 H   But no comma separates adjectives when they are not
        independent — that is, when they cannot be reversed with-
        out making the sentence sound unnatural.

> no comma
> ↓
> I have a new stereo recording of *The Rite of Spring*.

No one would say "a stereo new recording."

19

Quotations and Quotation Marks

---

19 A   Quotation marks are used to indicate the actual words of a speaker.

"I wonder," speculated the judge, "whether you have cited all the facts."

---

19 B   The first word of a direct quotation is capitalized if that quotation is a complete sentence.

↓

The judge then grew angry and remarked, "This is a court of law, not an arena for rhetoric!"

---

19 C   When the quotation comes after a verb of *saying* or *thinking,* a comma separates the introductory words from the quotation.

↓

Then we could hear the judge mutter to himself, "This nonsense has gone far enough!"

---

19 D   When the quotation comes before the verb of *saying* or *thinking,* a comma precedes the closing quotation mark.

↓

"I will have no more disturbances," the judge remarked patiently.

19 E   If the quotation ends with a question mark or an exclamation point, that comma is omitted.

no comma
↓

"I will have no more disturbances in this court!" the judge roared.

no comma
↓

"Do you realize the magnitude of your crime?" asked the judge.

---

19 F   When a quotation is interrupted within a sentence, commas precede and follow the interruption, and capitals are not used when the quotation resumes.

no capital

"What in the world," remarked the judge, "are you trying to prove?"

no capital

"The evidence is inconclusive," remarked the judge, "and I'm dismissing the case."

but

"The evidence is inconclusive," remarked the judge. "The case is closed."

The last sentence uses a period because there is no conjunction to connect the two thoughts.

---

19 G   The question mark, the exclamation point, and the dash come within the quotation mark when they are part of the quotation; otherwise they appear after the quotation mark. All periods and commas come within the quotation mark. The semicolon and colon come after the quotation mark.

I have just finished Poe's "The Black Cat."

Have you read Poe's "The Black Cat"?

Laura has just finished reading "The Black Cat"; her reaction
was decisive: "What an amazing story!"

What an amazing story is Poe's "The Black Cat"!

She called the story "amazing," and she suggested that we all
read it.

I enjoyed "The Black Cat": it absolutely fascinated me.

---

19 H   Single quotation marks are used when a quotation appears within another quotation.

The judge stared at the witness and coldly remarked, "But you
specifically said, 'The phone was off the hook,' didn't you?"

And then we heard the remark, "I'll bet no one knows who
said, 'My kingdom for a horse!'"

---

19 I   When material of four or more lines is quoted, that material is put into block quotes — that is, it is separated from the text, indented, and single-spaced. Quotation marks are not used unless someone is actually speaking within that block quote.

We are accustomed to think of Mark Twain's world as an essentially comic one, and we often regard his world view as an optimistic one. But there is a side to Twain that is far less assuring. In *The Mysterious Stranger*, for instance, he describes the persecution of an innocent woman:

> They hanged the lady, and I threw a stone at her, although in my heart I was sorry for her; but all were throwing stones and each was watching his neighbor, and if I had not done as the others did it would have been noticed and spoken of. Satan burst out laughing.

The Satan that Twain refers to is the voice of objectivity throughout the novel. Satan constantly chides the protagonist of the novel to look at the world the way it is, not the way the protagonist would like it to be:

"What an ass you are!" he said. "Are you so unobservant as not to have found out that sanity and happiness are an impossible combination? No sane man can be happy, for to him life is real, and he sees what a fearful thing it is. Only the mad can be happy, and not many of those. The few that imagine themselves kings or gods are happy, the rest are no happier than the sane."

---

19 J A quotation mark that appears at the end of a *sentence* indicates that the speaker has stopped speaking. If a quotation mark immediately begins the next sentence, a new speaker is speaking.

The encounter between Apollo and Hermes is a good illustration of the type of conflict the ancient gods got involved in.

"Do you know anything about my cattle?" inquired Apollo.
"Of course not," answered Hermes.
"I think you're lying."   [Apollo]
"How could I be lying? After all, what do I know about cattle? I'm just a baby."   [Hermes]
"Yes, but a shepherd clearly stated that it was a baby who was leading a herd of cattle from my pasture."   [Apollo]

---

19 K When a quotation extends for several paragraphs, quotation marks are used at the beginning of every paragraph that continues the quotation. An end quotation mark is not used until the speaker stops speaking, no matter how long the speech is and no matter how many paragraphs the speech uses.

When a quotation from a poem is incorporated into the text, a slash mark (/) indicates the end of the poem's line. If the first word of the next line is capitalized in the poem, it is also capitalized in the quotation.

Duncan realizes that appearances are deceptive. In fact, he remarks that "There's no art/To find the mind's construction in the face." Still, he naïvely trusts Macbeth and in the next scene warmly greets him.

When several lines of poetry are quoted, they are indented and reproduced exactly as they appeared in the original poem.

Duncan realizes that appearances are deceptive. In fact, his observations are painfully ironic:

> There's no art
> To find the mind's construction in the face.
> He was a gentleman on whom I built
> An absolute trust.

MISCELLANEOUS USES OF THE QUOTATION MARK

19 M Whereas the names of long works of writing are italicized, the names of short works or of sections within longer works are usually put in quotation marks: names of poems, chapter titles, short stories, articles in magazines, titles of essays, and so on.

The first section of Dickens' *A Tale of Two Cities* is called "Recalled to Life." "The Shoemaker" is the concluding chapter to this section.

19 N Quotation marks should not be used to express irony, disapproval, or the fact that a word is being used in an unusual sense. Such quotation marks often indicate that a writer is apologizing for the use of a particular word or phrase. If writers have reservations about a word, they should not use that word.

The "professionals" that support Laetrile are mostly quacks.

It would have been better to be direct:

The so-called professionals that support Laetrile are mostly quacks.

19 O   When a quoted phrase is incorporated directly into a sentence without an introductory word of *saying* or *thinking*, there is no need to capitalize.

The Constitution specifically states that the President's salary "shall neither be increased nor diminished" while he is in office.

---

19 P   No special punctuation is needed for an indirect quotation.

Anita told me that the play was spectacular.

Each of the following sentences uses incorrect punctuation:

Anita told me "that the play was spectacular."

Anita told me that "the play was spectacular."

Anita told me that, "The play was spectacular."

Anita said: the play was spectacular.

The following sentence, however, is correct:

Anita said, "The play was spectacular."

20

The Colon

---

20 A The colon introduces items in a series.

There are four countries I would like to visit: India, China, South Africa, and Egypt.

---

20 B The colon should not be used unless there is a word that indicates a series, and it should not be used after the verb *to be*.

no colon
↓
The four countries I want to visit are India, China, South Africa, and Egypt.

The treaty had two stipulations: that neither country should obtain military assistance from Russia and that each country should abide by the terms of the Geneva Convention.

but

no colon
↓
The treaty stipulated that neither country should obtain military assistance from Russia and that each country should abide by the terms of the Geneva Convention.

---

20 C The colon is often used instead of a period to indicate that a reason or an explanation is following.

I knew that she cared for me: when I was in the hospital she visited me every day.

The colon in the above sentence indicates a cause and effect relationship that could have been expressed:

I knew that she cared for me because, when I was in the hospital, she visited me every day.

---

20 D   The colon can introduce a long or a formal quotation.

Eisenhower's belief about the nature of power is to my mind particularly apt: "As long as there are sovereign nations possessing great power, war is inevitable."

---

20 E   Capitals do not usually follow a colon even if the words after the colon form a complete sentence. An exception to this practice, however, occurs when the colon introduces a direct quotation.

Our bluff has been called and we will respond: we must fight.

The words of the President were devastating: "We must fight."

21

The Question Mark and Exclamation Point

---

21 A   If a question appears within another question, only one question mark is used.

Who knows the answer to this question: "What is the capital of Minnesota?"

---

21 B   When the question mark or exclamation point appears within dashes or parentheses, no capital is used when the parenthetical sentence appears within another sentence.

It took ten years—did you realize that?—for the treaty to be negotiated.

---

21 C   The question mark and exclamation point come within the quotation mark when they are part of the quotation. Otherwise, they appear outside the quotation mark.

Have you read "The Lottery"?

Have you read "Why Was Maisie Sad?"

And then the judge remarked, "Are you sure you understand what perjury is?"

Why did the judge say, "I think that there is some perjury in this room"?

21 D   When a question mark or an exclamation point concludes a quotation, no comma follows.

"I will not serve!" exclaimed Satan.

"Why are you so hostile?" asked the judge.

21 E   Question marks and exclamation points should not be used to express sarcasm, irony, or disapproval.

What a charming (!) thing to say about a friend.

Thank you for your objective (?) remarks.

The marks in parentheses should be deleted and the disapproving attitude made more direct.

21 F   Multiple question marks or exclamation points do not strengthen the emotion of a sentence. In fact, multiple marks are a sign of immaturity—at least in formal writing.

That was dumb!!!!

Won't you ever learn???

Delete all but one mark in each sentence.

21 G   Either a comma or an exclamation point can follow a mild interjection. If the exclamation point is used, the next word is capitalized.

Aha! Now I know who is responsible.

Aha, now I know who is responsible.

21 H   A question mark can be used either with or without parentheses to indicate that a piece of information is uncertain.

The lifetime of Julius Caesar, 100 B.C. (?)–44 B.C., was one of great political turbulence.

The lifetime of Julius Caesar, 100?–44 B.C., was one of great political turbulence.

---

21 I   Question marks can be used after each item in a series to stress the various items.

While you were in Europe, did you visit the Roman Forum? attend any services at the Vatican? hear any concerts in Salzburg? walk along the Seine?

22

The Dash

22 A The dash indicates a change in thought within a sentence. It is often used to set off extraneous information, a side comment, an explanation, or some parenthetical expression.

The character of Mephistopheles—this is one of the many names for the devil—appears in art, literature, and music throughout the past five hundred years.

And then—and you probably won't believe this—we got into another accident.

22 B When an expression is within dashes, even if that expression is a complete sentence, the first word is not capitalized and there usually is no terminal punctuation. The only terminal punctuation marks used within dashes are the exclamation point and the question mark. The opening word is still not capitalized, however.

And then the people all took stones—are you sure that you haven't read the story?—and threw them at the victim.

22 C The dash is sometimes used to emphasize a word or a group of words, especially an appositive.

One goddess in particular took no nonsense from either man or god—Hera.

Lincoln, Coolidge, Truman—these three were highly controversial during their respective terms of office.

22 D   The dash can indicate that a thought is incomplete. A period is not used after an incomplete thought; a question mark or exclamation is permissible if either is required by the sense of the fragment.

He looked up sadly: "I saw what happened when they — "
He looked up sadly: "Did you see what happened when they — ?"

22 E   In current usage, a comma is not used either before or after a dash.

no comma
↓

As soon as the signal was given — and it was given promptly at

no comma
↓ ↓
noon — the workers left their jobs.

23

Parentheses

---

23 A   Parentheses enclose supplementary information, qualifying expressions, or side comments that the writer does not want to emphasize.

The reasons for the economic recession will be cited later (see Chapter 4); first, however, I want to define the extent of the recession.

---

23 B   A complete sentence enclosed within parentheses does not begin with a capital letter nor end with any punctuation mark other than an exclamation point or question mark if that parenthetical sentence lies within another sentence.

no capital
↓

There are many reasons for the recession (they will be listed

no period
↓

later), and they are complex ones.

---

23 C   However, when the parenthetical information rests outside any other sentence, it is treated as a normal sentence.

There are many reasons for the economic recession. (Chapter 4 will list most of them.) For now, I wish to focus upon the extent of the recession.

23 D   Parentheses are used to cite specific textual references.

The scene in front of the corpse (III,ix) is perhaps the most brilliant scene in the novel. Emma Bovary is lying in state while the mourners indulge in petty quarrels.

The allusion here reminds us of that ominous statement: "Dust you are, and to dust you shall return" (Genesis 3:19).

Macbeth has relinquished his membership as part of the human race:

> I dare do all that may become a man;
> Who dares do more is none.   (I,vii,46 – 47)

And indeed it is clear, even at this point in the play, that he will do more.

---

23 E   While there are established conventional situations in which parentheses are justified, parentheses are often abused and, in fact, are often unnecessary. Most of the types of information put into parentheses would have been more appropriately incorporated directly into the text.

WEAK: If one is going to talk about the nature of evil (a subject that has been heavily treated by philosophers throughout the ages), one ought to tell the story of Andvari's ring (unfortunately a complex and boring story) and of the many people who suffered because of that ring.

IMPROVED: If one is going to talk about the nature of evil, a subject that has been heavily treated by philosophers throughout the ages, one ought to tell the story of Andvari's ring and of the many people who suffered because of that ring. It is a complex and boring story, but it does clearly illustrate the fact that evil strikes without favoritism both the good and the bad.

24

Brackets

---

24 A   Brackets are used within a quotation to indicate words that are not part of the quotation; thus, brackets often enclose explanatory material within a quotation.

---

24 B   Brackets should not be interchanged with parentheses. Whereas parentheses enclose supplementary statements by the speaker, brackets enclose supplementary statements by someone other than the speaker.

Carlyle's belief that "history [is] a distillation of rumor" is one that we should not forget.

Carlyle's original words were: "History a distillation of rumor."

"You will see from the public journals [that] we have begun to reform, and that we are trying to cleans [*sic*] the Augean stables, and to expose to view the corruption of the agents of the late [i.e., of John Quincy Adams's] administration."

The middle part of this quotation by Andrew Jackson might also have been expressed:

". . . and that we are trying to cleans[e] the Augean stables. . ."

25

Ellipsis Marks

25 A Three dots indicate an ellipsis—that is, the fact that words have been omitted.

Let me quote from the Constitution: "New States may be admitted by the Congress into this Union; but no new state . . . shall be formed by the junction of two or more states . . . without the consent of the legislatures of the States concerned." Article IV, Section III—shall I read it again?

25 B Note that when the ellipsis marks come after a complete thought, a fourth dot is used to express the end period.

Surely all of you will remember those famous words: "Fourscore and seven years ago our forefathers brought forth on this continent a new nation. . . ."

But when the ellipsis marks indicate an obviously incomplete thought, only three periods are needed.

Surely all of you will remember those famous words: "Fourscore and seven years ago. . ."

25 C Ellipsis marks sometimes indicate hesitation or deliberativeness or ask the reader to pause for a moment.

I expect nothing from you . . . nothing but your best, that is.

Additional information concerning the use of ellipsis marks is presented in Chapter 33.

26

The Hyphen

There are very few absolute rules governing the hyphen. Its use is largely a matter of taste and judgment. Its three most important functions are to indicate that two or more words are functioning together, to avoid ambiguity, and to indicate that a word is divided between two lines. The following types of expressions are hyphenated:

26 A Compound expressions — that is, two or more words being used as one word or one idea:

the wine-dark sea to get a hot-foot
a 440-yard dash a twelve-pound baby
Mr. Know-it-all himself open- or closed-minded
Next in succession is the 59-year-old Andres Fortin.

26 B Compound words beginning with *self* and *ex,* and compounds beginning with *pre, post, anti,* and *pro* where the second element is capitalized or a figure:

the ex-governor anti-American post-Romantic period
self-motivated pro-American pre-1900

26 C Fractions, and numbers from twenty-one to ninety-nine:

five hundred fifty-fifth one-sixteenth of a pound

26 D   Possibly ambiguous expressions:

a slow moving-van   a slow-moving van
five pound-bags   five-pound bags

26 E   Words that are divided into syllables:

con-sti-tu-tion-al-i-ty

26 F   Note the following abuses of the hyphen:

a) Words of one syllable cannot be divided. *Through,* for instance, cannot be divided.

b) When a word is divided, you must be able to pronounce both parts of the division. The division of *telepho-ne* is incorrect because *ne* has no separate sound. The division should have been *tele-phone.*

c) When the first word of a compound expression is an adverb in *-ly,* that expression is not hyphenated.

an overtly hostile message

d) If a compound expression used as an adjective follows the noun it modifies, then the expression is not hyphenated.

an earth-shattering discovery

but

The discovery was earth shattering.

a well-stocked store

but

The store was well stocked.

Again, it should be emphasized that the uses of the hyphen as cited in this chapter are not rules but conventions, and some writers will ignore these conventions if they feel they can do so without creating ambiguity. If you are in doubt whether to hyphenate an expression, check a dictionary.

27

Italics

If you want to indicate that a word or phrase should be put in italics, merely underline that word or that phrase in your manuscript. The following types of expressions are italicized:

27 A   Names of books, magazines, newspapers, plays:

Time magazine   the Washington *Star*   *The Cocktail Party*

27 B   Names of vehicles, such as the name of a ship, rocket, airplane:

the *Queen Mary*   the rocket ship *Enterprise*

27 C   Names of works of art and music:

Beethoven's *Emperor* Concerto   the *Mona Lisa*
Rodin's *The Thinker*

27 D   Foreign words and expressions:

It's a *fait accompli,* I'm afraid.
Our partnership has worked because we have maintained a *quid pro quo* relationship.

27 E   Numbers, letters, and words used as words rather than
        for their meaning:

        The *5*'s on your typewriter aren't clear.
        There are four *fives* in 5555.
        The word *independent* has three *e*'s.
        I can't tell whether that is a *4* or a *9*.

27 F   Words or phrases that you want to emphasize — but do
        this very sparingly:

        As far as I could tell, it made no difference what you *did;* it's
        who you *were* that counted.

27 G   Sometimes you may want to italicize a word that is al-
        ready within an italicized expression. In such a case, indi-
        cate the distinction by using regular type:

        Keller's book *The Inspiration behind* War and Peace *and Other
        Napoleonic Novels* is not very interesting.

        Some writers will use quotation marks instead of italics.
        Other writers will disregard most of the uses of italics
        that this chapter has cited. While neither of these prac-
        tices is recommended, you should be aware that consider-
        able variation may exist in matters of style.

28

The Apostrophe

28 A   The apostrophe indicates that a letter has been omitted.
It appears at the point where the letter has been deleted.

isn't – is not   fishin' – fishing   the mid-'60s
'mediat'ly – immediately

Contracted words are common in dialect:

An' you're jus' tryin' t' be orn'ry.

28 B   The apostrophe indicates possession.

the boy's = of the boy   [one boy]
the boys' = of the boys   [of more than one boy]
James' or James's = of James

28 C   When there is joint possession, the final possessor gets the
apostrophe.

Mary, Martha, and Mildred's room   [The room belongs to the
three of them.]

28 D   When there is separate possession, each of the possessors
gets an apostrophe.

Mary's, Martha's, and Mildred's clothes

[The clothes are owned separately, not jointly.]

28 E   Remember (Section 6 A) that the possessive form of the personal, interrogative, and relative pronoun does not take an apostrophe.

its   whose   ours   theirs   yours   hers   his

28 F   The apostrophe indicates the plural of numbers, letters, symbols, and words used as words.

You have too many *and*'s in your sentence.
I can't tell your *8*'s from your *S*'s.
Did you get any *C*'s this term.
The paper was full of ***'s.

Note: Some writers do not use the apostrophe after numbers:

the 1930's   *or*   the 1930s

29

Numbers

29 A Hyphenate fractions and numbers from twenty-one to ninety-nine.

two-thirds   two hundred thirty-five
thirty-three and one-third

29 B Write out numbers expressed in one or two words except numbers in dates, addresses, page references or numbers with symbols such as $, %, ¢, and a decimal point.

On June 6, 1980, twenty-three representatives met to discuss the proposed $2.4 million tax-package.

If there are both long and short numbers in a passage, express all the figures in numeral form.

There were 35 representatives from Virginia, 328 from Florida, and 103 from Alabama.

29 C Avoid beginning a sentence with numerals. Either write out the number or rephrase the sentence so that the numeral does not come first. Instead of

755 people came to the meeting last Thursday.

say

Last Thursday 755 people came to the meeting.

29 D When a number is used as a word rather than for its numerical worth, underline (italicize) it. Add *'s* to make it plural.

There are three *3*'s in 333.

---

29 E   Ordinal numbers are usually written as words: *first, second, third,* etc.

---

29 F   Numerals are used with *A.M. (a.m.)* and *P.M. (p.m.);* words are used with *o'clock.*

twelve midnight   12 A.M.   eight o'clock
12:15 a.m.   twelve-fifteen in the evening

---

29 G   The points cited above are not rules but conventions, and these conventions are not absolute. Some writers will use numerals where others will use words. Some writers will not use an apostrophe to express the plural of a numeral. The use of words as opposed to numerals is often a matter of taste. In formal writing that is not technical, the frequent appearance of numerals is unattractive. In formal writing, the mode of expression is the word, and words should be used unless there is a good reason for using a numeral.

30

Abbreviations

30 A   When an abbreviation ends a sentence, only one period is used.

I enjoy most team sports: soccer, basketball, baseball, etc.

30 B   When the following abbreviations are used within a sentence, a comma separates them from the words that follow. There is always a punctuation mark — either a comma, a dash, or a parenthesis — in front of the abbreviation.

etc.   (*et cetera:* and so forth)
et al.   (*et alii* or *et alia:* and others)
i.e.   (*id est:* that is, namely, that is to say)
e.g.   (*exempli gratia:* for example)
viz.   (*videlicet:* namely)

I visited the usual sights in Athens, such as the Parthenon, the Temple of Hephaestus, the law courts, etc., and then I went down to Crete.

The presidents that we have been talking about — i.e., Washington and Lincoln — were pioneers.

30 C   Notice in the two examples above that when the sentence continues after the abbreviation, a comma follows the period of the abbreviation.

. . . the law courts, etc., and then . . .
— i.e., Washington and Lincoln

30 D   While it is permissible to abbreviate a common title in front of a proper name — Dr. Briger, Mr. Linn, Mrs. Martin — it is not proper to abbreviate most titles. One would not say, for instance, Pres. Carter or Sen. Childs. Nor would one ever abbreviate a title without a proper name. It is equally improper to abbreviate ordinary words, such as words of measurement, weight, money, distance, time, or amount.

IMPROPER: On Jan. 8, 1980, Dr. and Mrs. Henderson announced the birth of a 6 lb. son. The Dr. is associated with Del. Com. Hospital.

REVISED: On January 8, 1980, Dr. and Mrs. Henderson announced the birth of a six-pound son. The doctor is associated with the Delaware Community Hospital.

---

30 E   Do not use a symbol when a simple word exists.

I lost several dollars [*not* $'s] in the game.

For a glossary of abbreviations, see Chapter 39.

31

Capitalization

The following statements about the use of capital letters are not absolute. There are variations in the use of capitals just as there are variations in the use of other mechanical elements and in the use of punctuation. Rather than to memorize a set of rules, a writer should try to understand the reasons behind the rules. In fact, the word *rules* is itself inaccurate; the word should be *conventions*, and the writer should realize that the conventions do change.

Most uses of capitals fall into one of two general categories: to indicate the beginning of a sentence and to indicate a specific name or title.

31 A   Specific names together with their titles and corresponding abbreviations are capitalized.

a) Names of people:

Dr. Adam Greene   Governor Andrew Walter
General David Hill   Senator Amy Foster

b) Names of places:

Portland, Oregon   the Virgin Islands
35 Center Street   the World Trade Center

c) Names of organizations and institutions:

Antioch College   Community High School
General Electric   the Girl Scouts of America
the Democratic Party   a Baptist
the New England Conservatory of Music

d) Names of specific vehicles:

the *Titanic*	the *Merchant Queen*
the *Enterprise*	*Discovery II*
the S.S. *Constitution*	the Orient Express

e) Names of languages:

French   Swahili

f) Names of specific days, months, periods of time:

Saturday   January   Labor Day   the Middle Ages

g) Words formed from proper nouns:

Canadian literature	Indian mythology
an Edenic existence	a Dantesque experience

---

31 B   Many words are capitalized when they refer to a specific person, place, or thing. When they do not refer to something specific, they are not capitalized.

Lancaster Street	the street where I live
Mayor Brian Rogers	the mayor of Indianapolis
Modern History is a difficult course.	I enjoy reading modern history.
Coach Ashby	Mr. Ashby, the basketball coach
Aunt Sarah	my aunt in Texas
the Senior Class	He is a senior.

---

31 C   Similarly, titles of honor are not capitalized when they come after the name of a person.

President George Sampas of Trinity College

Mr. Sampas, the president of Trinity College

---

31 D   Titles of specific high-ranking officials are usually capitalized when they substitute for a specific person.

the President	the Pope	the Chief Justice
the Prime Minister	the Queen	the Secretary of State

But when these titles refer to no one in particular, they are not capitalized.

No American has ever been pope.

Her dream is to become president of this country.

---

31 E   The seasons – summer, winter, fall, autumn, spring – are not capitalized.

---

31 F   *North, South, East, West* are not capitalized unless they refer to a specific geographical region. They are not capitalized when they refer to direction.

He lives in the Deep South although he was born in the Far East.

Drive south for three miles and then turn west.

Most of the museums are in the southern part of the city.

---

31 G   Capitalization of titles of books, movies, articles, etc., is idiosyncratic. The usual practice is to capitalize all major words: nouns, pronouns, adjectives, adverbs, verbs. Capitalized also are the first and last word of the title and prepositions of more than four letters.

Gone with the Wind   The Mill on the Floss
Portrait of the Artist as a Young Man

---

31 H   The names of the planets are capitalized. There seems to be no agreement nowadays as to whether to capitalize the name of the planet earth.

Mercury is closer to the sun than Earth.

Jean Foucault proved that the earth revolves around the sun.

CAPITALIZATION OF SENTENCES

31 I   Every sentence begins with a capital letter.

31 J   Capitals are not used when a complete sentence is within parentheses or dashes, included within another sentence.

I will tell you more — ↓people have written books on the subject — if you want to hear it.

I will tell you more (↓people have written books on the subject) if you want to hear it.

31 K   But capitals are used when a complete sentence in parentheses is not a part of another sentence.

Most wars are useless. (↓Some people would say that all wars are useless.) They illustrate man's basest instincts.

31 L   When a direct quotation is a complete sentence, the first word of that quotation is capitalized even when the quotation lies within another sentence.

It was Archimedes who said, "↓Give me a place to stand and I will move the earth."

31 M   When the quotation is interrupted in the middle of the

sentence, capitals are not used when the quotation resumes.

"Give me a place to stand," said Archimedes, "↓and I will move the earth."

---

31 N   Capitals do not usually follow a colon unless the colon is introducing a direct quotation.

We realized our only course of action: ↓we would have to escape.

Mr. Beran's words were decisive: ↓"We will succeed."

32

Spelling

English spelling is ghastly; it is often inconsistent, capricious, and unpredictable. Nonetheless, there are some rules that can help remove some of the seeming arbitrariness of English spelling.

WORDS THAT END IN -e

32 A   Drop the final -e when you add a syllable that begins with a vowel.

intrigue: intriguing   intrigued
live: living   lived
debate: debating   debated   debatable
use: using   used   usable   usage
refine: refining   refined
bride: bridal
compute: computation   computed   computable

If a verb ends in -ie, change that -ie to a -y when you add -ing:

tie   tying
lie   lying
die   dying

32 B   Keep the final -e when you add a syllable that begins with a consonant.

refine – refinement   lone – lonely
waste – wasteful   nine – ninety

Exceptions: truly, awful, wholly, argument

---

32 C   When you add *-able* or *-ous,* keep the final *-e* after the letter *-g* if the *-g-* is pronounced like a *-dj-* and after a soft *-c-* (as in *cent*).

knowledgeable   changeable   courageous
advantageous   noticeable   serviceable

---

32 D   Adjectives that end in *-able* form the adverb by changing the final *-e* to *-y.*

capable – capably   noticeable – noticeably

WORDS THAT END IN *-y*

---

32 E   If a word ends in a consonant + *y,* form the plural of nouns and the third person singular of verbs by dropping the *-y* and adding *-ies.*

baby – babies   consistency – consistencies
cry – cries   try – tries

Exception: Keep the *-y* in the plural of proper names.

There are three *Cathys* in the office.

---

32 F   If a word ends in a consonant + *y,* change the *-y* to an *-i* when you add endings. But keep the *-y* if the ending begins with an *-i.* In other words, never have *-ii-.*

baby: babied   babying   babyish
reply: replied   replying   replier   replies
lonely: lonelier   loneliest   loneliness
cry: cried   crier   crying
necessary: necessarily

32 G   If a word ends in a vowel + *y*, keep the *-y* and merely add the endings.

buy: buys   buying   buyer
play: plays   playing   player   played   playable

32 H   Always add *-ly* to the adjective form of the word, never to the noun form.

not   *accident-ly*   but   *accidental-ly*
not   *occasion-ly*   but   *occasional-ly*
not   *incident-ly*   but   *incidental-ly*

WORDS ENDING IN A CONSONANT

32 I   Form the plural by adding *-s.*

girl – girls   dog – dogs

A compound expression forms its plural by making plural the noun of the expression or the most important word:

sister-in-law   sisters-in-law
five-year-old   five-year-olds
commander in chief   commanders in chief
passer-by   passers-by
lady in waiting   ladies in waiting
governor-elect   governors-elect
looker-on   lookers-on

32 J   Form the singular possessive by adding *-'s* and the plural possessive by adding *s'*.

girl's = of one girl   girls' = of more than one girl

Form the possessive of a compound expression by adding *-'s* to the last word:

sister-in-law's (singular)   sisters-in-law's (plural)

32 K   If the word ends in an -*s*, a -*z*, or an -*x*, form the plural by adding -*es*.

fox – foxes   mess – messes   bus – buses

Note: Words ending in -*s* or -*z* sometimes double that -*s* or -*z* before the -*es*. Hence,

bus – buses *or* busses   fez – fezzes

---

32 L   If the word ends in an -*s*, a -*z*, or an -*x*, form the possessive singular by adding -'*s* or by adding a single apostrophe.

the fox's prey   *or*   the fox' prey
Louis' sister   *or*   Louis's sister

Note: The -'*s* form is usually preferred.

Form the plural possessive by putting an apostrophe after the -*s* of the regular plural ending.

the foxes' victims   the buses' fumes

---

32 M   If a word ends in a consonant/vowel/consonant — for example, hit, spar, admit — and if the final syllable of that word is the accented one, then the final consonant is doubled when you add an ending beginning with a vowel.

spit:	spitting	spitter	
hit:	hitting	hitter	
occur:	occurring	occurred	occurrence
admit:	admitting	admitted	admittance
rob:	robbing	robbed	robber	robbery
refer:	referring	referred	referral

But *reference* has only one -*r*- because the final -*r*- is no longer part of the accented syllable. The word is pronounced *ré ference*, not *refer' ence*.

Notice *commit – committing – committed* but *commitment*. The reason *commitment* does not double the -*t*- is that the suffix (-*ment*) does not begin with a vowel.

WORDS ENDING IN -ion

---

32 N   Words in *-te* go to *-tion:*

relate – relation
arbitrate – arbitration

---

32 O   A vowel + *t* goes to *-ssion:*

omit – omission
remit – remission
commit – commission

---

32 P   A consonant + *t* goes to *-sion:*

convert – conversion
invert – inversion

WORDS WITH *-ie-* AND *-ei-*

---

32 Q   Write *-ei* after the letter *-c-* or when the sound is pronounced *-ā-*.

after *-c-:*   conceive   perceive   receipt
pronounced *-ā-:*   neighbor   freight   weight   sleigh

Otherwise, write *-ie-*. Note that the sound here is *-ē-*.

piece   niece   believe   chief   yield

Exceptions:

either   neither   leisure   weird   seize
height   foreign

Summary of Plural and Possessive Forms

Word	Singular possessive: usually just add 's	Plural	Plural possessive: put apostrophe after final -s of plural; otherwise -'s
brother	brother's (32 J)	brothers (32 I)	brothers'
brother-in-law	brother-in-law's (32 J)	brothers-in-law (32 I)	brothers-in-law's
passer-by	passer-by's (32 J)	passers-by (32 I)	passers-by's
dome	dome's (28 B)	domes	domes'
lady	lady's (32 J)	ladies (32 E)	ladies'
Nancy	Nancy's (32 J)	Nancys (32 E)	Nancys'
chimney	chimney's (32 J)	chimneys (32 G)	chimneys'
Smith	Smith's (32 J)	the Smiths (32 I)	the Smiths'
boss	boss's or boss' (32 L)	bosses (32 K)	bosses'
gas	gas's or gas' (32 L)	gases (32 K)	gases'
box	box's or box' (32 L)	boxes (32 K)	boxes'
child	child's (32 J)	children (irregular)	children's
wife	wife's (32 J)	wives (32 R)	wives'
Mr. Walters	Mr. Walters's or Mr. Walters' (32 L)		
the *Tribune*	the *Tribune*'s		
basis		bases (32 T)	
criterion		criteria (32 T)	
an *A*		several *A*'s (28 F)	
1900		the 1900's or the 1900s (28 F)	

WORDS ENDING IN -*f* AND -*fe*

32 R Words ending in -*f* or -*fe* often (but not always) form their plural by changing the -*f* to -*ves*.

half – halves   wife – wives   life – lives   leaf – leaves

WORDS ENDING IN *-sede, -cede, -ceed*

32 S *Supersede* is the only verb that ends in *-sede. Proceed, succeed, exceed* are the only verbs spelled *-ceed*. Other verbs are spelled *-cede:*

precede   intercede   concede   accede   recede

FOREIGN WORDS

32 T Words from the Latin and Greek often keep their original endings.

-us,	singular	*-i*, plural	alumnus – alumni
-um,	singular	*-a*, plural	memorandum – memoranda
			agendum – agenda
			curriculum – curricula
			addendum – addenda
-is,	singular	*-es*, plural	crisis – crises
			analysis – analyses
			basis – bases
			thesis – theses
-on,	singular	*-a*, plural	criterion – criteria
			phenomenon – phenomena

32 U A few warnings:

a) Be alert to homonyms – that is, words that are pronounced the same but have different meanings – for example:

course – coarse   cereal – serial   principal – principle

or to words that are very close in pronunciation, for example:

personal – personnel   conscious – conscience

b) Be alert to the fact that there is sometimes a difference between American spelling and British spelling.

British:	flavour	colour	centre	cheque	defence
American:	flavor	color	center	check	defense

c) When you are in any doubt about the spelling of a word, always consult a dictionary.

32 V   The following list contains perhaps the most frequently misspelled common words in the English language. They are embarrassingly common words, but it is a rare person who can spell all of them correctly.

absence	criticize	laboratory	referring
accidentally	dealt	leisure	replies
accommodate	decided	license	resistance
accustomed	decision	loneliness	responsibility
achievement	definitely	maintenance	rhythm
acquaint	dependent	mandatory	schedule
across	description	manufacturer	seize
address	develop	mathematics	sense
aggravate	different	monotonous	separate
aggressive	disagreement	necessary	similar
agreement	disappear	neither	sketch
alcohol	disappoint	no one	source
a lot	disgrace	noticeable	speech
among	dormitory	occasionally	succeed
amount	either	occurrence	successful
anonymous	embarrassing	omission	supposed to
apartment	environment	omitted	surprise
apparent	equipment	opinion	temperature
appearance	equivalent	optimism	tendency
argument	exaggerate	organization	together
article	excellent	particularly	tomorrow
around	existence	perform	tragedy
athletic	experience	personal	tried
basically	explanation	phenomenon	truly
beginning	familiar	physical	unanimous
believe	finally	possession	unconscious
benefited	forty	precede	until
business	gauge	prejudiced	used to
challenge	guarantee	prerogative	usually
character	guard	pretension	vicious
clothes	harass	privilege	weird
committee	height	probably	whether (or not)
comparative	hindrance	procedure	whose (of whom)
competent	immediately	proceed	who's (who is)
competitive	independently	proportion	
congratulate	innocence	psychology	
conscience	interesting	pursue	
conscious	irritate	quantity	
corollary	it's (it is)	quarter	
courteous	its (of it)	receive	

33

Quoting

Since writing, particularly nonfiction, often deals with the statements and ideas of others, it is important to indicate the source of those statements and ideas. You can incorporate the source into your writing by paraphrasing:

Furthermore, war tends to dehumanize the participants. Thomas Bailey suggests that prolonged fighting weakens the ethics of the combatants.[1] Such dehumanization was clearly illustrated in the Viet Nam conflict.

or you can incorporate the writer's words directly into your writing:

Furthermore, war tends to dehumanize the participants. Thomas Bailey remarks that "where fighting is protracted and uncivilized, the ethics of combat are ordinarily pulled down to a more primitive level."[1] Such dehumanization was clearly illustrated in the Viet Nam conflict.

Regardless of which approach you use, you should acknowledge that the idea is not yours, and you should identify your source. The technicalities of crediting sources in footnotes will be explained later.

PLAGIARISM

Writers often wonder what they should footnote. Does every fact have to be footnoted? The answer is no, not

---

[1] Thomas A. Bailey, *The American Pageant* (Lexington, Mass.: D. C. Heath and Company, 1971), p. 604.

every fact. It is not necessary to credit a source for facts that are generally available, that are part of one's fund of general knowledge. It is not necessary, for instance, to credit a source for the fact that Custer and his men were annihilated on June 25, 1876, at Little Bighorn; but if a source referred to this defeat as "the most embarrassing debacle in fifty years" and you were to quote this opinion, you would have to acknowledge your source.

It is necessary to footnote the following:

a) an opinion of someone else

b) an original idea or observation of someone else

c) a line of thought that has been suggested or inspired by someone else

d) specialized facts — facts that have been obtained from one particular source

e) the words of someone else, regardless of whether those words have been used verbatim or have merely been paraphrased

In short, you must be honest. You should not claim as your own what you have gotten from someone else. You should be very careful in presenting information to distinguish your own words and ideas from the words and ideas of others. Failure to give proper credit is plagiarism, a criminal offense in scholarship.

Here is an example of plagiarism:

Original source:

What Steinbeck is saying in "The Snake" is that, while we can shut ourselves off from certain instincts or emotions (such as love, sex, attraction toward others), such an isolation is unnatural. These instincts or emotions can enter most subtly and, when they do enter, we can be totally thrown off guard and off balance. Man was not meant to live alone. Hence, one of the ironies of the story is that, while Dr. Phillips was engaging in experiments concerning nature, his own life was an unnatural one. He engaged in experiments without understanding the implications of what he was doing. Life and death, sex and reproduction, were things he could not respond to emotionally. Again, note the emphasis at the beginning of the story to his lack of feeling and sensitivity: at one moment he's killing a cat; then he's petting another cat; then he's eating supper nonchalantly. Steinbeck seems to be suggesting that such a life is unnatural.

Example of plagiarism (the plagiarized material is underlined):

Another concern in Steinbeck's works is the need for community and companionship. The Joad family in *The Grapes of Wrath* are strong as long as they are together; but when the family begins to break up, the morale of the individual members of the family begins to disintegrate. Steinbeck's short story "The Snake" illustrates the same concern. Here, the protagonist, Dr. Phillips, has isolated himself to such an extent that he has forgotten how to feel. Steinbeck is saying that such an isolation is unnatural. He is suggesting that human beings are social beings and that it is not right for them to live alone.

The first underlined phrase is lifted from the original. The second phrase merely changes a few words: "Man was not meant to live alone" becomes "it is not right for them to live alone." Finally, note that the paragraph as a whole is too close to the original source. The inspiration for the entire passage seems to come from the original.

Now, there is nothing wrong with incorporating the ideas of someone else, but credit must be given for those ideas. All the writer needs to do is to identify in a footnote what the source of the inspiration was.

INCORPORATING QUOTATIONS

As we noted previously, whenever you use the words or ideas of another source, you must acknowledge that you are quoting. If the material that is quoted is relatively short—three lines or less—then simply incorporate the quotation into your essay:

One must be very careful when using the word *traitor* or *treason;* it is improper to use these words loosely. The Constitution specifically states that a person cannot be convicted of treason

33

"unless on the testimony of two witnesses to the same overt act, or on confession in open court." Therefore, to use the words merely to express one's strong disapproval is highly unprofessional.

If the material to be quoted is relatively long – four lines or more – then put that material in block quotes. When you put material in block quotes, quotation marks are not used – unless, of course, someone is speaking within that block quote or unless the quotation is itself quoting some other source; see example on page 177.

There are some technicalities to follow when you quote from another work. The following itemizes most of those technicalities.

Original source:

A certain old man of the sea has his haunts here, immortal Proteus the Egyptian, who spends all his time in these waters; he is acquainted with the depths of the whole sea and is always most elusive. The servant of Poseidon, spending all his mornings tending Poseidon's seals, he sleeps in the afternoons, and that is the time to try to catch him. He can foresee the future, but he will use every trick at his disposal to evade you. If you wish to learn the future, sneak up upon him as he sleeps and hold him down. He will change his shape from water to beast to fire, but if you hold on long enough, he will weary and return to his normal shape, and give an answer. Because of the frequent contact with the seals, he is unusually smelly.

---

33 A   No direct quotation used:

Among the mythological predicters of the future was Proteus, whom Homer calls evasive and smelly.

---

33 B   **When you omit a word or a series of words from an original source, indicate that omission with ellipsis marks:**

There are many personages in Greek mythology who could predict the future. One of the most famous was Proteus. Homer describes him as "immortal Proteus the Egyptian, who . . . is

Another point concerns the use of the word

treason. It is important to realize that the word

is a precise one. Article III, Section II of the

Constitution is specific:

> Treason against the United States shall consist
> only in levying war against them [i.e., the
> United States], or in adhering to their enemies,
> giving them aid and comfort. No person shall be
> convicted of treason unless on the testimony of
> two witnesses to the same overt act, or on
> confession in open court.

Thorndike's analysis of this constitutional

point has been controversial for a long time, and

debate has not ceased. His analysis centers upon

the word "enemies":

> ". . . or in adhering to their enemies" has
> seemed to be an ambiguous phrase to some
> legislators, but in the context stated here, it
> must refer to both declared and undeclared
> enemies. Formal declaration of war is not the
> only criterion, or even a necessary criterion.[7]

Thus, Thorndike would admit as a traitor not only

someone overtly guilty as Julius Rosenberg but also

someone like Driscoll Faberson, who gave military

secrets to France, a country with which we were at

peace.

---

[7] William N. Thorndike Jr., Constitutional Law
(Washington, D.C.: C. Johnson Co. Inc., 1952),
p. 332.

acquainted with the depths of the whole sea and who is always most elusive."

---

33 C When the omission occurs at the beginning of a sentence, indicate the omission by inserting the ellipsis marks and then by continuing the sentence without capitalizing the first word:

There are many personages in Greek mythology who could predict the future. One of the most famous was Proteus. ". . . he is acquainted with the depths of the whole sea," says Homer in the *Odyssey*.

---

33 D When the omission includes the end of the sentence, supply a fourth dot to serve as a period:

Homer describes Proteus as follows: "A certain old man of the sea has his haunts here, immortal Proteus the Egyptian. . . . He can foresee the future, but he will use every trick at his disposal to evade you."

---

33 E Include any punctuation from the original source that may come before the ellipsis:

"The servant of Poseidon, spending all his mornings tending Poseidon's seals, . . . he is unusually smelly."

---

33 F When you include explanatory information, put that information in brackets:

"A certain old man of the sea has his haunts here [i.e., the eastern Mediterranean], immortal Proteus the Egyptian."

---

33 G When you italicize, indicate in brackets that the italics are yours. Put the brackets right after the italicized word:

". . . he will use *every* [italics mine] trick at his disposal," says Homer.

---

33 H   If you have more than one italicized phrase, establish that the italics are yours by indicating so in parentheses at the end of the paragraph. The following example illustrates this technique, as well as most of the other techniques just described:

There are many personages in Greek mythology who could predict the future. One of the most famous was Proteus. Perhaps Homer's description of him from Book III of the *Odyssey* is the best:

A certain old man of the sea has his haunts here [Homer most likely means the eastern Mediterranean], immortal Proteus the Egyptian, who . . . is acquainted with the depths of the *whole* sea and [who] is *always* most elusive. The servant of Poseidon, . . . he can foresee the future, but he will use every trick at his disposal to evade you. If you wish to learn the future, sneak up upon him as he sleeps. . . . He will change his shape from water to beast to fire, but if you hold on long enough, he will weary and return to his normal shape. . . . (Italics mine)

34

Footnotes

Footnotes are used to identify a source. They can also be used to insert explanatory material that otherwise might interrupt the flow of writing. The following specimen illustrates some of the range of footnotes:

[1] Eric Voegelin, *Plato* (Baton Rouge: Louisiana State University Press, 1966), p. 92.

[2] This observation was suggested by Gregory Katsas in *Plato's Allegories* (London: D. Chester, Ltd., 1979), Chapter 3.

[3] The context seems to suggest that *philos,* not *agape,* is the motivation. Voegelin agrees.

[4] Cf. a similar analogy in the *Gorgias,* 503c.

Some instructors will discourage the use of footnotes to contain explanatory material and will require that footnotes be used only to indicate sources. If you have any question about this practice, you should check with your instructor.

If you are preparing a manuscript for publication, the *MLA Style Sheet* cites specific guidelines concerning not only the presentation of footnotes but also the presentation of bibliographies, the preparation of a manuscript, and the handling of various mechanical elements. Since the MLA guidelines are so widely accepted, the following discussion of footnotes and bibliography by and large conforms to those guidelines. Needless to say, it would be very worth your while to have the *MLA Style Sheet* available if you plan to write an extensive research paper or article.

It should be noted that there are other styles for presenting footnotes. While the MLA is the self-appointed authority within the disciplines of modern languages and humanities, it is not always appropriate for psychology, political science, law, and so on. Much more widely accepted for all disciplines (except perhaps the sciences) is the *Manual of Style* published by the University of Chicago Press.

There are various ways to present footnotes. The common approach of all styles, however, is to present the author's name, the title, publication information, and textual reference.

The following is the conventional procedure for indicating a source the first time that that source appears in the footnotes:

---

34 A   For books – first entry:

a) author's full name as it appears on the title page; if there is more than one author, connect the final name with *and*

b) comma after final name

c) title of book (underlined)

d) comma and edition number if title page cited an edition number: 3rd ed.

e) open parenthesis

f) city of publication; if city is not easily identifiable, include the state as well

g) colon

h) name of publisher exactly as it appears on the title page, followed by a comma and the year of publication

i) close parenthesis followed by comma

j) textual reference followed by period: p. 89.
                                     pp. 237 – 40.

(for a work in more than one volume) III, 282.

---

34 B   For articles – first entry:

a) author's full name; if there is more than one author, connect the final name with *and*

b) comma after final name

c) full title of article in quotation marks; put comma before the closing quotation mark

d) name of publication in which article appeared; underline name of publication; follow by comma

e) publication information – date or volume number – followed by comma:

August, 1980,
Winter, 1979,
28 Sept. 1975,
20 (1968), [= Volume 20, published in 1968]
17, No. 9 (1978), [= Volume 17, No. 9, published in 1978]

f) textual reference (be as specific as necessary: page, column) followed by period:

p. 13.
pp. 13 – 16.
p. 3, col. 2.
p. 3, cols. 2 – 3.

Note: the *MLA Style Sheet* suggests that the abbreviation for page(s) be omitted if the publication information has cited the volume number:

20 (1968), 13.
20 (1968), 13 – 16.

---

34 C   Additional entries:

The footnote listings just cited apply to the first appearance of a source in the footnotes. When a source is repeated, abbreviated references indicate that repetition.

a) If two or more consecutive footnotes cite the same source, there are two different ways to indicate the repetition.

i) Merely write *Ibid.*, followed by the proper page number(s):

[1] Allan Moore, *The Western Pageant* (New York: P. C. Peeters, Inc., 1980), p. 391.

[2] *Ibid.*, p. 413.

ii) Repeat the author's name, followed by the proper page number(s):

² Moore, p. 413.

Select either style (i) or style (ii) and be consistent with that style. Do not use style (i) on one page and style (ii) on another.

b) If a footnote repeats a source that has been cited earlier and is not a consecutive listing, merely write the author's last name followed by the proper page number, as described in a) ii) above.

c) If you are using two sources by the same author and are repeating one of these sources, just cite the author's last name and the first key word or words of the title, followed by the proper page number(s):

⁵ Moore, *Western,* p. 452.

d) If there is no author listed, merely begin the footnote with the title.

---

34 D   The specimen footnotes shown on page 185 include most of the common features of citing references. The entries are fictitious, designed merely to illustrate the various technicalities. An explanation of each footnote appears on page 184.

---

34 E   Note the following additional points:

a) There is no period after the upraised footnote number when it appears either in the text or in the footnotes.

b) When the footnote number appears in the text, there is no space between it and the word or punctuation mark that it follows. When the number appears in the notes, however, there is one space between it and the first word.

c) Each word of a title is underlined separately, not continuously.

d) Every footnote ends with a period.

1   Footnote for a book—perhaps the most common type of footnote.

2   Indicates same source as the previous one—i.e., Camp's *Middle Ages;* note different page reference, however.

3   A signed article in an encyclopedia.

4   A signed article in a periodical.

5   A book with more than three authors.

6   Indicates the same Camp source as listed earlier—refers us back to footnote 1.

7   A book that has been edited rather than authored; if there had been just one editor, the abbreviation would have read *ed.*

8   A second book by Camp.

9   An unsigned article in a periodical.

10   A book that has been translated and revised.

11   Since Camp has two citations in the bibliography, it is now important to specify which of the two works is being referred to.

12   Another reference to the article first cited in 9.

13   An unsigned entry in an encyclopedia.

14   A periodical in which volume number has been cited.

15   A work quoted from another work.

1 William John Camp, <u>The</u> <u>Middle</u> <u>Ages</u>, 3rd ed.
(New York. Harper and Row, 1976), p. 92.

2 <u>Ibid</u>., pp. 98–101.

3 Anita P. Rogerson, "Charles II," <u>Encyclopedia</u>
<u>of</u> <u>European</u> <u>Royalty</u>, 7th ed. (Chicago: The Bowmar
Co., 1970), III, 272. Unless otherwise specified,
all information on Charles II is taken from this
source.

4 Sherman Baldwin, "The New Royalty," <u>Time</u>, 8
Nov. 1977, p. 62.

5 Danielle Santander Downing <u>et</u> <u>al</u>., <u>The</u> <u>Great</u>
<u>Monarchs</u> (Newark, N.J.: The Dart Press, 1965),
p. 213.

6 Camp, p. 108.

7 Kedrick Burgess Carr and John David Greene,
eds., <u>Crucial</u> <u>Editorials</u> (Muncie, Indiana: The
Potter Publishing Co. Inc., 1980), pp. 15–16.

8 William John Camp, <u>The</u> <u>Dark</u> <u>Ages</u>, 2nd ed.
(Springfield, Ill.: The Sundown Company, Inc.,
1973), p. 813.

9 "Good News Amid the Gloom," <u>Time</u>, 1 Nov. 1976,
p. 52.

10 William Henry Foster III, <u>The</u> <u>Mind</u> <u>of</u> <u>the</u>
<u>Renaissance</u>, trans. and rev. Jeremy H. Guth (Paris:
Hachette, 1966), p. 342.

11 Camp, <u>Middle</u> <u>Ages</u>, pp. 110–112.

12 "Good News," p. 52.

13 "Boxer Rebellion," <u>Encyclopedia</u> <u>Britannica</u>,
1972 ed., Vol. II, pp. 207–208.

14 Thomas D. Everett, "A Declining Era," <u>PMLA</u>, 92
(1970), 1080.

15 René Descartes, <u>Principia</u> <u>Philosophiae</u> (Paris,
1644), cited in Christopher Giuliano, <u>Descartes</u>
(Baltimore: Forbes Publishers, 1972), p. 82.

Page number at top center of page; could have been put in upper right-hand corner.

No space before upraised footnote number.

Example of quotation directly incorporated into text.

Quotation marks not needed because writer is citing a fact, not someone else's opinion, idea, or direct words.

Note that the typed text is double spaced.

Note also the wide margins on both the right and left sides of the paper.

Block quotes for long quotations; indented four spaces from left margin; block quotes always single spaced, not double spaced; quotation marks not used.

Brackets denote an insertion of the writer of the paper.

A 1½-inch line separates text from footnotes; double space above and below this line.
Footnote illustrates a source being mentioned for the first time.

Ibid. refers to the same source as the previous footnote.

Footnotes begin four spaces to the right of the margin; one space between upraised footnote number and first word; if note continues beyond one line, all subsequent lines begin at left margin, not indented.

Shortened form of reference to a work that has already been mentioned.

4

of the century. She was born of aristocratic parents, people who "knew that they were better than their equals and acted accordingly,"[6] and these parents made every effort to seclude her from what they considered undesirable influences. She rarely left the confines of the family manor; hence, she grew up a "virtual prisoner in a peopleless paradise."[7] She did enter St. Matthew's Hospital in 1917 for an osteotomy[8] and she did attend St. Hilary's School from 1919 to 1921, but otherwise she rarely left home. "People simply were not part of her youth. She was aware that they existed . . . but she regarded them no more than she regarded an elm on the manor grounds."[9] Indeed, even her work and her style at St. Hilary's reflected this unconcern:

> She was always alone. It is true that the school was a boarding school and that a contact with peers was unavoidable. Still, she managed. . . . Her essays were about ideas and sometimes about things; the characters were merely implementors or spokesmen for those ideas. In fact, . . . one character could rarely be differentiated from another; they all acted and sounded the same. Old Muttonchops [this was the nickname for her father] could sometimes be identified, but otherwise the people were merely puppets.[10]

This lack of concern with people was evident in her first novel, Time Without End, written in 1935. Only two characters appear in this novel, a seventeen year-old girl and her father. There is frequent dialogue between these two characters, but it is clumsy and amateurish.

---

[6] Gregory P. Duff, The Decline of the Aristocrat (London: W.J. Westchester, Ltd., 1974), p. 218.

[7] Ibid., p. 235.

[8] John Gerard Hart, Jr., Elizabeth Bowerdon: A Study in Silence (Boston: The Groves Press, 1972), p. 35. Unless otherwise specified, all information about Bowerdon's youth comes from this source.

[9] Duff, p. 242.

[10] Hart, pp. 117-118.

e) The beginning of a footnote is indented four spaces to the right.

f) If the footnote continues onto the next line, the note continues at the far left margin.

g) A space should be skipped between each footnote and the next.

h) Footnotes can appear collectively at the end of the paper or at the bottom of each page in the text. The second procedure is better for the reader.

---

34 F Page 187 illustrates a typical page of a research paper in which the footnotes appear at the bottom of each page.

---

34 G Finally, it should be recognized that the procedures just cited for writing footnotes are not absolute. Some manuals of style will say that there should be no space between the footnote number and the beginning of the footnote; others will suggest that there be no line between the text and the footnotes; others will say that the name of the publisher should not appear in the footnotes; others will say that periods instead of commas should be used to separate the author from the work and the work from the publisher; others will say that the volume number should follow the title of a book that has more than one volume; some will say that footnotes should always appear on the same page as the text; others will say that the footnotes should always appear at the end of the paper.

What is important is that you be consistent with whatever style of presentation that you do use. If one footnote separates the author from the title with a comma, then all other footnotes must do the same. The *MLA* guidelines are always safe ones, but if for some reason you choose to vary them, be consistent with your variation.

35

Bibliography

The format of the bibliography involves as many technicalities and as much care (and fussing) as does the format of footnotes. As with footnotes, consistency is important in setting up the bibliography. You can make minor alterations to the conventions, but you must be consistent with those alterations. For instance, consider the following two presentations:

Roberts, Mark Jason, *A Local Centennial,* 3rd ed. New York, The Randolph Company, 1979.

Roberts, Mark Jason. *A Local Centennial.* 3rd ed. New York: The Randolph Company, 1979.

The first one uses commas where the second uses periods. Whichever style is chosen must be used consistently.

The bibliography should include every work that you used either directly or indirectly in the preparation of your research paper. Even if you did not use a particular source in your footnotes but did use that source in preparing your research, you should include that source in the bibliography since it is possible that the source had some influence upon your thinking even without your realizing that influence.

Here are some of the conventions used in citing a work in a bibliography:

35 A   Last name of author appears first; if there is joint authorship, names of other authors appear in normal order with

period after final name; if there are more than three authors, merely write the name of the first author to appear on the title page and follow that name with *et al.*

---

35 B Cite title of work — names of books are underlined; names of articles are put in quotation marks — followed by a period.

For books

---

35 C Add ancillary information if there is any, followed by period:

3rd ed.	[= 3rd edition]
6 vols.	[= 6 volumes]
Ed. Clifton York.	[= edited by Clifton York]
Trans. Willard Gardiner.	[= translated by Willard Gardiner]
Rev. Allan Moore.	[= revised by Allan Moore]

---

35 D Publication information: name of city followed by colon followed by name of publisher followed by comma followed by date of publication followed by period.

For articles

---

35 E Name of periodical (underlined) followed by comma.

---

35 F Publication information — date or volume number — followed by comma:

August, 1980,
Winter, 1979,
28 Sept. 1977,
20 (1968),   [= Volume 20, published in 1968]
17, No. 9 (1978),   [= Volume 17, No. 9, published in 1978]

35 G   Page reference(s), followed by period.
      Again, the MLA guidelines suggest not using *p.* or *pp.*
when a volume number has been cited:

20 (1968), 29 – 30.

but

28 Sept. 1977, pp. 24 – 26.

Other conventions

35 H   If two entries are by the same author, do not repeat the author's name. Merely indicate repetition of the same name by a raised line of about a half inch.

35 I   If the entry runs to more than one line, indent all subsequent lines four spaces.

35 J   Every entry appears in alphabetical order, whether that entry begins with the name of an author or with the title of an article.

35 K   Each entry ends with a period.

35 L   Articles from encyclopedias, newspapers, and periodicals include page references. Books do not include page references.

35 M   Be sure to skip a line between each entry.

35 N   The bibliography should begin on a fresh page.

The following specimen bibliography includes most of the common features of a bibliography. The entries, as was the case for the entries of footnotes, are fictitious, designed merely to illustrate specific principles.

BIBLIOGRAPHY

Aristotle. <u>The Posterior Analytics</u>. Trans. Maria
    Aviado. Boston: M. Smith & Co., 1978.

————. <u>The Prior Analytics</u>. Trans. John
    Rhinelander. Chicago: Wood, Prince, and Scott,
    Inc., 1976.

Baldwin, Sherman. "The New Royalty." <u>Time</u>, 8 Nov.
    1977, p. 62.

"Boxer Rebellion," Encyclopedia Britannica, 1972,
    II, 207-8.

Camp, William John. The Dark Ages. 2nd ed.
    Springfield: The Sundown Company, Inc., 1973.

————. The Middle Ages. 3rd ed. New York: Harper
    and Row, 1976.

————, and David Hill. An Introduction to the
    Renaissance. Rev. Christopher Dorn. Boston:
    The Sentinel Company, 1980.

Carr, Kedrick Burgess and John David Greene, eds.
    Crucial Editorials. Muncie: The Potter
    Publishing Co., Inc., 1973.

Downing, Danielle Santander, et al. The Great
    Monarchs. Newark: The Dart Press, 1965.

Everett, Thomas D. "A Declining Era." PMLA, 92
    (1970), 1080.

Foster, William Henry, III. The Mind of the
    Renaissance. Trans. and rev. Jeremy H. Guth.
    Paris: Hachette, 1966.

"Good News Amid the Gloom." Time, 1 Nov. 1976,
    p. 52.

Rogerson, Anita P. "Charles II," Encyclopedia of
    European Royalty. 7th ed. Chicago: The Bowmar
    Co., 1970, III, 272.

Sampas, George. A Treatise on Pollitiks [sic].
    First published in London, 1672.

Webster's New World Dictionary of the American
    Language. Cleveland: The World Publishing
    Company, 1966.

Wiley, Steven R., President, T.R.S. Research and
    Development. Personal Interview. Concord,
    Massachusetts, 30 Dec. 1979.

————. "The Economic Determinants of Politics."
    Lecture delivered at Harvard University,
    Cambridge, Mass., 7 Aug. 1976.

Wray, Charles G. Aristotle's Influence in 16th
    Century French Politics. Unpublished doctoral
    dissertation, University of Massachusetts, 1972.

36

Manuscript Preparation

Whenever you submit a piece of professional writing to another person—regardless of whether it be the final draft of a paper, a thesis, an article for publication, a letter of introduction or application—you should remember that you begin making an impression upon your readers as soon as they look upon the printed page. An unprofessional appearance can make your readers less receptive to what you have to say. A sloppy appearance may give readers the impression that you are careless, that you are amateurish, that you really don't care very much, or that you are complacent, and your readers may question your competence even before they begin reading. An employer who sees a letter that looks amateurish may never bother to read the letter but may summarily discard it. Therefore, as superficial as it may seem, the appearance of the copy that you submit is important. The following criteria are standard ones:

---

36 A   Whenever possible, type. Typed copy is not only a courtesy to the reader; it is a professional convention.

---

36 B   Be sure that your ribbon is dark, that your touch is firm and even, and that the typewriter keys are clean so that the impression upon paper will be a clear and distinct one.

36 C   Use standard $8\frac{1}{2} \times 11$ inch paper; it should be either white or only slightly off-white.

36 D   Provide margins: at least an inch at the right and at the bottom; about two inches from the top; and about an inch and one-half at the left.

36 E   Type on only one side of the paper.

36 F   Double space all manuscript copy. Single space all letters; be sure that there is a double space between paragraphs.

36 G   Leave two spaces before beginning a new sentence; be sure that there is a single blank space after any internal mark of punctuation.

36 H   Proofread meticulously. Be sure that no words have been omitted, that all words have been correctly spelled, and that the conventions of punctuation and mechanics have been honored.

36 I   If you have to make corrections, make them discreetly. Corrections should not be obvious to the reader. If you find that you have made several corrections on the page, it is best to scrap that page and to retype. The final copy

should be as clean as possible. Avoid submitting any pages that have scratch-outs, smudges, or words inserted by hand.

---

36 J   If for some reason you have to write instead of type, always use ink — preferably a fountain pen to a ball-point pen. The ink should be black or dark blue. The paper in manuscripts can be lined; in letters it should be unlined.

THE FORMAL LETTER

In addition to the criteria listed above, the following conventions should be observed when you write a professional or a business letter — that is, a formal letter:

---

36 K   If you are using stationery without a letterhead, be sure to supply your return address. This information appears at the upper right-hand corner of the page. The date usually appears as the last item in the return address; if your stationery already has a letterhead, the date is located underneath it.

---

36 L   Include the full title and address of the person to whom you are writing. This information is located a few spaces below the last item of the return address and to the far left-hand margin. If more than one line is needed for any particular item, indent the second line three spaces to the right:

Mrs. Jennifer Hildreth
Director of Management and
   Personnel Services
Trafalgar Publications, Inc.
102 West 78th Street
New York, N.Y. 10024

Mr. Adam Greene, Treasurer
Hyland, Porter, and Sons
4040 North Walker St.
Indianapolis, Indiana 46205

If you prefer end punctuation, include it consistently:

Mr. Adam Greene, Treasurer,
Hyland, Porter, and Sons,
4040 North Walker St.,
Indianapolis, Indiana 46205

It is more common nowadays not to use end punctuation.

---

36 M   The salutation should include a title: Mr., Mrs., Dr., Senator, etc. A colon follows the person's name if you want to be formal or if you do not know the recipient personally. If you wish to be less formal or if you do know the recipient, a comma follows the person's name.

---

36 N   If the letter is short, center the text on the page. A letter in which all the content is located on the top half of the page is unattractive and looks silly, and if it looks silly, the reader may not take it as seriously as you intend.

---

36 O   Paragraphs may or may not be indented; current usage is divided. If you do indent, the indentation should be about five spaces to the right.

---

36 P   The complimentary closing (Yours truly, Sincerely yours, etc.) appears a few spaces after the last line of the letter

toward the right-hand margin. The first word of the complimentary closing is capitalized; subsequent words are not. A comma follows the last word.

---

36 Q   The letter should have both a written and a typed signature. The typed signature is under the written one. If your letter suggests a response, you might want to include your telephone number under your typed name.

---

36 R   The letter should be folded into thirds along the 11-inch side; it should be mailed in a standard 9 × 4 inch envelope.

The following specimen illustrates the conventions of a formal letter.

323 75th St.
Apt. 7-B
Chicago, Ill. 60654
March 13, 1980

Mr. Michael Ward
The Salisbury Press
602 Madison Avenue
New York City 10022

Dear Mr. Ward:

I am sending under separate cover a copy of the
three short stories that you requested. I have
also included the synopsis for a story that is now
in progress.

Since you seemed eager to see these stories, I did
not take the time to retype them, although I did
make some alterations on the manuscript itself. If
you feel that any of the pages should be retyped, I
will be glad to oblige.

Meanwhile, let me thank you for expressing an
interest in my work. I will be glad to meet with
you at your convenience.

                              Yours truly,

                              Eleanor Atkins

                              Eleanor Atkins
                              (312) 772-9806

glossaries

37

Fine Points: Diction and Usage

English usage is often picky and idiosyncratic. There are fine points and subtleties. The following list includes some important information; it also includes some petty distinctions. Few people will fuss if you say *out of* or if you interchange *bring* and *take* or if you use *hung* instead of *hanged*. Nonetheless, if you value precision, you should be at least aware of these distinctions, no matter how petty they may seem. Certainly, in informal discourse you may wish to disregard some of these distinctions, but in formal writing you will want to be as precise as you can. Some of the information has already been mentioned in earlier chapters; it is repeated here for completeness.

accept – except   *Accept* is a verb; it means *to take, to receive.*
> I will accept your offer.

Except, a verb, means *to exclude, to exempt.*
> I will except you from attending the meeting.

Except, a preposition, means *other than, excluding.*
> Everyone except Bruce and Warren has arrived.

Except is not a conjunction. It is improperly used in the following sentence:
> Everyone was ready to go except the twins had not finished packing.

But or some equivalent conjunction should have been used, or an object can be supplied for the preposition *except:*
> Everyone was ready to go *except for* the twins, who had not finished packing.

adopt – adapt   *Adopt,* a verb, means *to accept, to take in.*
> We will adopt the recommendation. They adopted a child.

Adapt, a verb, means *to alter, to change from one shape or condition to another shape or condition.*

We will have to adapt to the new environment.

The play was adapted from a short story.

advance–advanced You advance through the ranks. You advance your theory. You get an advance on your salary. You give advance warning or notice.

You have advanced through the ranks. Your daughter is advanced for her years. You are in an advanced physics course.

adverse–averse *Adverse* means *unfavorable:* adverse publicity, adverse weather conditions. *Averse* means *unwilling.*

I am not averse to hearing your proposal.

advice–advise *Advice* is a noun; it rhymes with *ice.* One gives advice. *Advise* is a verb; it rhymes with *rise.* One advises someone.

affect–effect *Affect,* a verb: *to move emotionally.*

I was deeply affected by your performance.

Affect, a verb: *to influence.*

An intervening phrase does not affect the number of a verb.

Affect, a verb: *to put on an appearance.*

She tried to affect an air of elegance.

Effect, a verb: *to cause to happen, to bring about.*

Congress has effected many changes in foreign policy.

Effect, a noun: *a result, consequence, outcome.*

The new policies will have some subtle effects upon our lives.

aggravate *Aggravate* means *to make worse* or *to intensify.* Only in informal English does it mean *to irritate* or *to annoy.*

INCORRECT: I get so aggravated when I hear such gossip.

CORRECT: Scratching a wound will merely aggravate it.

agree You agree *with* a person. You agree *to* an idea, suggestion, or proposal.

allow *Allow* does not mean *concede* or *admit* in formal discourse. It means *to permit.*

INCORRECT: He allowed that he had been wrong.

CORRECT: He allowed the power of his position to weaken.

all ready–already The *all* in *all ready* means *all of.*

We are all ready to leave. = All of us are ready to leave.

Already is an adverb of time.

They have already finished their preparations.

all right – alright   *Alright* has traditionally been considered incorrect. Gradually, however, the word seems to be assuming a certain legitimacy, and some dictionaries are recognizing the word. It is still safer to use *all right* exclusively.

all together – altogether   *Altogether* means *completely, thoroughly.*

We were altogether outraged at his behavior.

Together means *in one group.*

We were all together for the first time in years.

allusion – illusion – delusion   An *allusion* is a reference.

The speaker made several allusions to classical myths.

An *illusion* is a deceptive appearance or a false belief.

The optical illusions were startling.

She was under the illusion that she would be elected to the committee.

A *delusion* is similar to an illusion but stresses even more strongly the folly of the belief.

They were under the delusion that they would triumph no matter what methods they used.

a lot   *A lot* is always written as two words, never as one word.

already   See *all ready.*

alright   See *all right.*

also   Do not begin a sentence with *also;* it is an adverb, not a conjunction. Use *in addition* or *furthermore* or an equivalent.

altogether   See *all together.*

amend – emend   When you amend, you make improvements. You can amend a document or you can amend your behavior. *Emend* is used specifically to refer to improvements that are made in a piece of writing.

among – between   *Between* is used to refer to two people or things.

Between the two of us, I think he's wrong.

Among is used with three or more people or things.

The reward was distributed among Jeb, Greg, and me.

Remember that *between* and *among* are prepositions. Consequently, a pronoun that follows one of these words must be in the objective case: not *between Katie and I* but *between Katie and me.*

amount–number *Number* is used with items that can be counted. It is usually used with plural nouns.

I have a number of things to do today.

Amount is used with items that cannot be counted. It is usually used with singular nouns. It refers to quantity.

The amount of gossip in this office is shameful.

analysis Use *analysis,* not *analyzation.*

angry You are angry *with* a person; you are angry *at* a thing, event, or action.

annoyed You are annoyed *with* a person; you are annoyed *at* a thing, or an action. In these two uses, the verb means *angered.* When *annoy* means *badger* or *irritate,* it is followed by *by:*

The camper was annoyed by the mosquitoes.

any Be sure to include *other* when you are comparing a member of a group to the group itself.

The Bruins are more colorful than any other hockey team.

any (in compounds) The following are always written as one word: *anything, anywhere, anybody, anyhow. Any more* is written as two words. The following can be written as one or as two words depending upon the context: *anyone/any one* and *anyway/any way.*

Ask anyone you want.

You can have any one gift.

I did not use your typewriter, but thanks anyway.

You can go any way you wish.

anyone, anything Be sure to include *else* when you are comparing a member of a group to the group itself.

Gregory is more forceful than anyone else on the debating team.

anyway Use *anyway,* not *anyways.*

anywhere Use *anywhere,* not *anywheres.*

apt–liable–likely *Apt* means *appropriate, suitable, qualified, naturally inclined.*

That was a wonderfully apt choice of words.

Geniuses are apt to be temperamental.

Her training makes her apt for the position.

Liable means *accountable* in an undesirable sense.

You are liable to get hurt if you play with explosives.

You are liable for all damages.

Likely merely indicates probability.

It is likely to stop raining soon.

as – like

a) *As* is a conjunction, equivalent to *in the way that.*

Jeremy was successful, as we might have predicted.

No one could play the piano as Josef Hofmann could.

b) *Like,* on the other hand, is a preposition, equivalent to *similar to.*

No one could play like Josef Hofmann.

c) *As* can be equivalent to *while* but not to *because.*

INCORRECT: As you arrived late, you cannot vote.

CORRECT: As I was driving, I became aware that something was wrong.

d) *As* should not be used in an indirect question. Use *whether.*

I don't know whether [not *as*] I will go.

e) *As* can be a preposition meaning *in the role of.*

Three students serve as members of the Executive Committee.

f) Use a subjunctive **after** *as if* and *as though* when the main verb is past.

He behaved as if he *were* a baby.

as to   Either omit the words or substitute *about.*

WEAK: He had many ideas as to what to do.

IMPROVED: He had many ideas about what to do.

at   Do not use *at* with the word *where.*

Where does he live at?

Simply delete the *at.*

at – with   A verb of emotion is followed by *with* plus a person or by *at* plus an idea, thing, event, act.

to be annoyed/angered/delighted with a person

to be annoyed/angered/delighted at a thing, act, event

averse   See *adverse.*

awake – wake   *Awake* means *to get yourself up. Wake* means *to get someone else up.*

I awoke at noon. I woke her up at noon.

a while – awhile   *Awhile* is an adverb. *While* is a noun.

Can you stay awhile? Can you stay for a while?

bad – badly   Use *bad* after the verb *feel* when the verb refers to your feelings rather than to your sense of touch.

I felt bad when I heard the news of the accident.

because Don't use *because* after the expression *reason is/was.* Use *that.*

> WEAK: The reason I was upset was because I had just received some bad news.

> BETTER: The reason I was upset was that I had just received some bad news.

> FINE: I was upset because I had just received some bad news.

being that, being as These two expressions are unacceptable in formal discourse. Use *because.*

beside – besides *Beside* means *next to, by the side of.*

> Whom is he sitting beside now?

Besides means *in addition to.*

> No one besides you and me knows about this.

> Besides a new car, he has a new house and a new boat.

between See *among.*

Bible The Bible is neither italicized nor put in quotation marks.

> I am trying to read the Bible from cover to cover. I am now at Luke 3:4.

black, white These words when they designate race are not capitalized.

> There seems to be a much better understanding nowadays between blacks and whites.

blame You blame someone *for* something. You do not blame something *on* someone.

breath – breathe *Breath* is a noun and rhymes with *death. Breathe* is a verb and rhymes with *seethe.*

bring – take Things are brought toward the speaker and taken from the speaker.

> Bring the books to me. Take the books to her.

but Use a gerund, not *but,* after *can't help.*

> I can't help wondering [not *but wonder*] what is going on.

but that Use *that,* not *but that,* after an expression of doubting.

> There was no doubt that [not *but that*] he would do what the sergeant ordered.

can – may *Can* denotes ability; *may* denotes permission.

You may publish my story if you make no changes.

Can you publish my story in the next issue?

can't help A gerund completes the meaning, not *but.*

I couldn't help thinking [not *but think*] that I had made a terrible mistake.

capital – capitol *Capital* is used in all contexts except for the name of a building:

the State Capitol Building   a capital suggestion

capital letters   Augusta is the capital of Maine.

We didn't have enough capital to buy the house.

censor – censure   *To censor* is to remove objectionable materials.

Before the movie was shown on television, it was censored.

To censure is to express disapproval.

The Congress decided to censure the President rather than to impeach him.

center You center *in* or *on* or *upon* something. You do not center *around* something.

The discussion centered upon the topic of forced busing.

cite – site *Cite* is a verb; it means *to identify, enumerate,* or *list.*

Cite five reasons for the U.S.'s involvement in World War II.

Site is a noun; it means a *location.*

Here is the proposed site for the new building.

chose – choose *Choose* is present tense; it rhymes with *cruise.*

Chose is past tense; it rhymes with *toes.*

clothes – cloths *Clothes* are garments; the word rhymes with *knows. Cloths* are pieces of fabric; the word rhymes with *moths.*

compare – contrast When you compare X *to* Y, you cite the similarities between X and Y. When you compare X *with* Y, you cite both similarities and differences between X and Y. When you *contrast* X with Y, you cite the differences between X and Y.

complacent – complaisant If you are *complacent,* you are smug, self-satisfied, content with the *status quo* and with glib responses.

The manager is so complacent that nothing ever gets done.

If you are *complaisant,* you are agreeable and eager to please.

Her complaisant manner has secured her many friends.

complement – compliment *Complement* is either a noun or a verb. Its root is the word *complete*. *Complement* refers to something that completes or that figuratively balances or that enhances.

> A good wine complements a meal.
>
> Salt and pepper complement each other.
>
> Vance is a good complement to Brzezinski: one is very cautious and the other quite candid.

Compliment, a noun or verb, expresses approval or praise.

> We complimented her for her performance.
>
> Our compliments made her blush.

comprise – compose – represent *Comprise* means *consist of, be composed of.* It takes a direct object.

> The novel comprises seven sections, and each section comprises seven chapters.

It is incorrect to say *comprised of,* as in

> The novel is comprised of seven chapters.

The proper idiom is *composed of:*

> The novel is composed of seven chapters.

Compose means *constitute, make up.*

> Three sections compose the novel.

Represent does not mean *make up, constitute,* as in

> Women now represent over 51 percent of the population.

To represent is to stand for someone else.

> Women constitute/compose over 51 percent of the population.
>
> Three women represented us at the convention.

contemptible – contemptuous *Contemptible* means *deserving contempt; contemptuous* means *feeling contempt.*

> Your behavior was contemptible.
>
> Your contemptuous attitude is partially justified.

continual – continuous *Continual* combines *frequent* with *off and on:*

> her continual nagging   his cóntinual bragging

Continuous means *constant:* the continuous sound of the waves

contractions Be sure to put the apostrophe where the letter has been omitted: *isn't* for *is not.*

convince – persuade To *convince* is to get someone to accept mentally. To *persuade* is to get someone to do something.

I tried to convince him that the idea was a good one.

I tried to persuade him to join us.

council – counsel A *council* is a group of people; it is a noun.

The School Council will be meeting this evening.

Counsel is a verb that means *to give advice to*. It can also be a noun meaning *advice* and a noun meaning *lawyer* or *advisor*.

He gave me good counsel.

Do you have legal counsel?

She counseled me when I was in trouble.

Does the counsel for the defense have any more questions?

credible – creditable – credulous *Credible* means *believable*.

Your story is quite credible.

Creditable means *worthy of praise*.

What a creditable performance!

Credulous means *believing too easily*.

I am not so credulous as to believe that story.

criterion – criteria *Criterion* is singular; *criteria* is plural.

data Technically, *data* is a plural word. However, since the singular *datum* has almost disappeared from the language, *data* is often used as a singular. If you are referring to obviously one piece of information, let *data* take a singular verb; if you are referring to obviously more than one piece of information, let *data* take a plural verb.

delusion See *allusion*.

demur – demure *Demur,* a verb, means *to hesitate* or *to have reservations*.

The chairman demurred at the thought of revising the proposal.

Demure is an adjective meaning *modest* and *serious*.

She is always so demure that I find it difficult to converse with her.

different *Different* is almost always followed by *from*. The only time that *than* is used is to connect clauses.

X is different from Y.

You are different from what I had expected.

You are different than I had expected.

discreet – discrete *Discreet* means *tactful, cautious,* and *careful* in one's words and actions.

Professional people must be discreet. An indiscreet remark can have serious repercussions.

Discrete means *separate, unrelated.*

Religion and literature are not discrete areas. There is much more of a relationship between them than you may realize.

disinterested – uninterested *Disinterested* means *unbiased, neutral.*

Let us take the advice of a disinterested third party.

Uninterested means *not caring, bored, lacking in interest.*

Let us hope that the jury will be disinterested, not uninterested.

divers – diverse *Divers* means *several.*

I hope that you will all bring your divers talents to this project.

Diverse means *different, various.*

I realize that you have all had diverse backgrounds.

doubt Expressions of doubting are followed by *that,* not *but that.*

There is no doubt that Pablo Picasso is one of the most important painters of the twentieth century.

due to Use *due to* after a noun or after the verb *to be.* Otherwise use *because of.*

His absence was due to illness.

He was absent because of illness.

Due to the fact that is wordy. Substitute *because.*

WORDY: Due to the fact that inflation is growing more rapidly than salaries, many people do not have enough money to buy what they used to be able to buy.

BETTER: Because inflation is growing more rapidly . . .

each

a) *Each* is regarded as singular when used as the subject of a sentence.

Each of the reporters *has* his or her assignment.

b) When *each* appears after a plural or a compound subject, the verb is plural; if the sentence has a complement, the complement is also plural.

The delegates each *have* their assignments.

Paul and Luke each *have* completed *their* reports.

c) When *each* (or *every*) comes before a compound subject, the verb is singular.

Each (Every) man, woman, and child *is* expected to enjoy the celebration.

effect See *affect.*

elicit – illicit *Elicit,* a verb, means *to draw out,* as to draw out a response.

> The chairman's outrageous suggestion elicited cries of horror from the members of the committee.

Illicit, an adjective, means *illegal, improper,* or *unlawful.*

> Such illicit behavior demands severe reprimand.

else See *anyone, anything.*

emend See *amend.*

eminent – imminent *Eminent* means *noteworthy* or *renowned.*

> He is a person of eminent wisdom.
>
> Let me introduce you to the eminent governor of Alaska.
>
> She is eminently qualified.

Imminent means *impending, likely to happen.* What is about to happen is often undesirable.

> I fear that war is imminent.
>
> imminent danger

equally *Equally* is not followed by *as.*

> INCORRECT: Dickens is equally as graphic as Hardy.
>
> CORRECT: Dickens is as graphic as Hardy.
>
> CORRECT: Dickens and Hardy are equally graphic.

erratic – sporadic *Erratic* refers to behavior. *Sporadic* refers to time.

> Her performance has been erratic. There are days in which she is excellent; on the other hand, there are days when she is terrible.
>
> She shows sporadic bursts of energy, but unfortunately she is not consistent.

etc. An abbreviation for *et cetera: and so forth.* There should be a comma before the abbreviation and, if the sentence continues, a comma after the period.

> When one argues, there are many emotions in operation, such as hostility, envy, etc., but perhaps the most important one is pride.

everyone – everybody *Everyone* and *everybody* are singular words. Do not be tempted to use a plural verb after them.

> Everyone *has* arrived on time.

exalt – exult *Exalt* means *to praise, to glorify.*

> The crowds exalted the king at his coronation.

Exult means *to rejoice.*

> Rita exulted at her election to the committee.

except See *accept.*

expect The verb means *to wait for, to anticipate, to look forward to.* It does not mean *to suppose* or *to suspect.*

INCORRECT: I expect that she simply overslept.

CORRECT: We expect them to arrive any minute now.

farther – further *Farther* refers to distance. *Further* refers to degree; it can be an adjective meaning *additional* or an adverb meaning *to a greater extent.*

We walked much farther than we had realized.

If there are any further developments, I will let you know at once.

I will pursue the matter further if you wish.

feel When the verb *feel* refers to feelings rather than to one's sense of touch, use an adjective, not an adverb, to complement it.

I felt bad when I realized that I had embarrassed you.

After *feel, well* serves as an adjective referring to good health.

I feel very well today.

fewer – less *Fewer* is used with items that can be counted; hence, it is usually used with plural nouns.

I have fewer things to do today than I had realized.

Less is used with items that cannot be counted; hence, it is usually used with singular nouns.

I have less freedom than I used to have.

flaunt – flout You *flaunt* when you show something off conspicuously.

He tastelessly flaunted his wealth.

You *flout* when you show disregard, often contemptuous disregard.

The participants of the Watergate affair flouted the law shamelessly.

flounder – founder When you *flounder,* you act awkwardly; you appear to be stumbling, confused, and unsure of yourself.

The guest speaker floundered badly throughout his talk.

Founder denotes a physical breakdown or collapse.

The horse foundered when it tried to jump the gate.

The ship foundered and sank.

former – latter *Former* means the *first of two; latter* means the *second of two.* Avoid using these words to express the first or the last in a series of three or more.

fulsome   *Fulsome* should not be used as a synonym for *extensive* or *great.* The word means *excessive,* often *insincerely excessive* or *offensively excessive.* Thus, *fulsome praise* has pejorative connotations.

gerund   Use a possessive before a gerund.

Your arriving late has inconvenienced all of us.

good – well   *Good* is an adjective; *well* is primarily an adverb.

His behavior was good. He behaved well.

After *feel, be, seem,* and other such linking verbs, *well* serves as an adjective meaning *healthy.*

It looks good enough to eat.   [not referring to health]

He looks well today.   [referring to health]

He looks good in his new suit.   [not referring to health]

half   The idiom is *half an X* or *a half X,* not *a half an X* or *a half of an X.* Merely remember not to use two *a(n)'s.*

hanged – hung   People are *hanged* when they are executed. Things are *hung* when they are suspended.

have   Always use *have,* never *of,* after *will, would, must, may, might, could, shall, should.*

We could have [not *of*] attended the conference if we had wanted to.

healthy – healthful   *Healthy* means *in a state of good health. Healthful* means *conducive to good health.* People are healthy. Foods and places are healthful.

hisself, theirself   These words are inappropriate. Use *himself* and *themselves.*

hypothesis – theory   People often use *theory* when they mean *hypothesis: I have a theory about the crime.* A *hypothesis* is an unproved theory, an idea, a speculation. A *theory,* on the other hand, is an idea based upon considerable evidence. A person who is merely speculating should say *I have a hypothesis about the crime.*

if – whether   *If* introduces a condition in which there are no alternatives.

What would you do if she agreed?

Whether indicates alternatives; the words *or not* are stated or implied.

Do you know whether she has agreed (or not)?

illicit   See *elicit.*

illusion   See *allusion.*

imminent See *eminent.*

imply – infer You *imply* when you suggest something. You *infer* when you draw a conclusion from someone else's words.

> I inferred from what you said that you were dissatisfied.
> The tone of your voice implies that you are dissatisfied.

in – into *Into* indicates motion toward; *in* indicates position.

> He went into the house. He is in the house.

ingenious – ingenuous *Ingenious* means *clever:* an ingenious suggestion/idea/plan. *Ingenuous* means *guileless, unsophisticated, straightforward, naïve.*

> It was refreshing to meet such an ingenuous person.

in regard to Say *in regard to,* not *in regards to.*

irregardless. The word is *regardless. Irregardless* is unacceptable.

its – it's – its' *Its* means *of it;* it denotes possession. *It's* is a contraction of *it is. Its'* doesn't exist.

it is + pronoun The formal expression is *It is I/he/she/they/we.* Informal usage, however, allows the more natural *It is me/him/her/them/us,* especially after the contracted form *it's.*

is because/when/where See *because, when, where.*

kind(s), sort(s), type(s) Do not mix singulars with plurals in expressions using these words.

this kind of gift	these kinds of gifts
this sort of idea	these sorts of ideas
that type of approach	those types of approaches

kind of, sort of These expressions do not mean *rather, quite,* or *somewhat.* They mean *a type of.* An expression like *I am kind of tired* should be avoided in formal discourse.

latter See *former.* Distinguish *latter* from *later. Latter* means the second of two; *later* refers to time.

lay – lie

a) *lie:* to tell a falsehood.

> I lie   I am lying   I lied   I have lied

b) *lie:* to be situated, to rest.

> I lie down   I am lying down   When I got home, I lay down
> I have lain down

c) *lay:* to put or place.

> I lay it on the shelf   I am laying it on the shelf

I laid it on the shelf   I have laid it on the shelf

lead – led *Lead* is present tense; it rhymes with *plead. Led* is past tense; it rhymes with *fled.*

lend – loan *Lend* is a verb; *loan* is a noun.

I will lend you my car.

I will repay the loan as soon as possible.

less See *fewer.*

liable See *apt.*

lie See *lay.*

like *Like* is a preposition meaning *similar to* or *such as.*

Performers like Vladimir Horowitz are exceptional.

See *as.*

like for instance *Like for instance* is careless.

Certain things irritate me, like for instance when people chew with their mouth open.

Merely delete the *like.*

Certain things irritate me – for instance, when people chew with their mouth open.

likely See *apt.*

loan See *lend.*

loath – loathe *Loath* rhymes with *both;* it means *unwilling, hesitant.*

I am loath to move too quickly on this proposal.

Loathe rhymes with *clothe;* it means *to dislike intensely.*

I loathe people who make sarcastic comments about others.

loose – lose – loosen *Loose* rhymes with *goose;* it means *free, untied,* and it is an adjective.

The lion is loose!

He is too loose with his money.

Lose rhymes with *dues.* It is a verb meaning *to mislay* or *to become separated from.*

Because of the scandal, Mr. Martin will certainly lose his position of leadership in this community.

Loosen is a verb meaning *to free* or *to untie.*

You may loosen your tie if you wish.

The chairman would not loosen his control over the activities of the committee.

may   See *can.*

momentarily – temporarily   If the main verb is future, use *momentarily:*

> We will return momentarily.

If the main verb is in the present tense, use *temporarily.*

> We are temporarily without transportation.

most   *Most* should not be used as a synonym for *almost,* as in *most everyone, most everything.*

myself   *Myself* is not a polite way of referring to yourself. Say *to me,* not *to myself.*

> She saw Harry and me [not *myself*] at last night's meeting.

need   When you use *need* as a third-person singular auxiliary verb, use *needs* if an infinitive follows; otherwise *need* is fine.

> All she needs to do is to consult the dictionary.

> All she need do is consult the dictionary.

never   *Never* should not be used as a synonym for *not yet. Never* indicates finality.

> INCORRECT: I never got around to finishing that book.

Strictly speaking, the only justification for the above sentence would be (a) if you were dead or (b) if the book no longer exists.

none   *None* can be either singular or plural.

> None of the letters are legible.

> None of the letter is legible.

notorious   *Notorious* is not a synonym for *famous.* A notorious person is indeed famous but for something toward which we have a disapproving attitude.

nowheres   *Nowheres* is an incorrect form of *nowhere.*

number   See *amount.*

of   This preposition is often unnecessary, especially after words like *inside, outside, off.*

one of those (these) X's who (that) . . .   The verb should be plural.

> She is one of those actresses that *stun* their audience.

If *only* precedes the expression, however, then a singular verb is used.

> She was the *only* one of the candidates who *was* qualified.

other   See *any.*

over with The *with* is unnecessary. It should be deleted.

passed – past *Passed* is a verb meaning *to go by* or any of the other many synonyms of *pass*.

> We passed our exit.   He passed away.   She passed out.

Past is an adjective meaning *over, former, previous* or a noun meaning a *former time.*

> The past decade was a turbulent one.

> You can never recapture the past.

personal – personnel *Personal* means *private. Personnel* has to do with one's employees.

> Don't ask me about my personal life.

> Mr. Byron is having trouble with his personnel.

persuade See *convince.*

phenomenon *Phenomenon* is singular; *phenomena* is plural.

plan An infinitive is preferable to a gerund after *plan.*

> *I plan to go* is preferable to *I plan on going.*

plenty *Plenty* is a noun, not an adjective. Therefore, such expressions as *plenty cold* and *plenty rich* are unacceptable.

plus *Plus* is not a conjunction; therefore, it should not begin a sentence or clause. Avoid sentences like this one:

> I was very tired. I had been traveling all day, plus I had not slept well the night before.

Substitute *furthermore, moreover,* or an equivalent conjunction.

precede – proceed *Precede* means *come before; proceed* means *move forward.*

prejudice – prejudiced *Prejudice* is a noun.

> She has a few prejudices.

Prejudiced is an adjective; it is usually followed by *against.*

> She is prejudiced against foreigners.

prepositions For the idiomatic use of prepositions, consult Chapter 12.

prescribe – proscribe *Prescribe* means *to advise, direct, order.*

> My itinerary has been prescribed in advance.

> The doctor has prescribed a month's rest.

> Our authority is prescribed by the constitution.

Proscribe means *to banish, forbid, outlaw.*

The ordinance proscribes smoking in public buildings.

principal – principle   *Principal* means *chief, main.*

the principal factors   the principal of a school
the principal plus the interest.

Principle refers to a standard of conduct or judgment.

It is the principle of the matter that I object to.

proceed   See *precede.*

prophecy – prophesy   *Prophecy* is a noun; it rhymes with *see.*

The prophecy was ominous.

Prophesy is a verb; it rhymes with *sigh.*

The oracle prophesied that a mighty kingdom would fall.

Note that the verb is *prophesy,* not *prophesize,* and that the past tense is *prophesied,* not *prophesized.*

prior to   *Prior to* means *before.*

proscribe   See *prescribe.*

quite   *Quite* means *entirely, completely,* not *rather* or *somewhat.*

quote – quotation.   *Quote* is a verb; *quotation* is a noun.

Alexandra quoted the Constitution; her quotation was a lengthy one.

Don't say *Her quote was a lengthy one.*

raise – rise   *Raise* means *to lift up* or *to increase;* it takes a direct object. *Rise* means *to move up* or *to be increased;* it does not take a direct object.

Lazarus was raised from the dead.

The banks raised the prime interest rate.

Prices are rising precipitously.

He has risen through the ranks.

rational – rationalize   *Rational,* an adjective, means *sensible, using one's reason. Rationalize,* a verb, means *to make excuses* for one's shortcomings, failures, negligence, etc.

Please be rational. Listen to what I am saying.

Please don't try to rationalize: you simply made a mistake.

You can try to rationalize your greed, but it's still greed.

re   *Re* is not an abbreviation; it is a remnant of the Latin word *re* (from *res*); it means *concerning, regarding, in regard to.* Sometimes one will see *in re.*

I am writing *re* your recent letter of application.

real   *Real* means *genuine,* not *very.* It is an adjective, not an adverb; therefore, statements such as *You are real clever* should be avoided.

reason . . . is because   See *because.*

represent   See *comprise.*

reverend   *Reverend* is an adjective, not a noun. Therefore, expressions such as *Reverend Childs* are inappropriate. There should be either a name or the word *Mr.* between the *Reverend* and the surname.

> the Reverend Edward Childs
>
> the Reverend Mr. Childs

rise   See *raise.*

for . . . sake

a) A proper noun before the *sake* uses the usual possessive form:

> for George's sake   for God's sake

b) A common noun does not use the usual possessive form when that possessive form would add an additional syllable; the apostrophe appears without the *-s:*

> for justice' sake
>
> for conscience' sake
>
> for change' sake

Using the usual possessive form (*-'s*) would increase the number of syllables. But

> for caution's sake
>
> for the king's sake
>
> for credibility's sake

Using the regular possessive form in these three examples does not increase the number of syllables.

seeing as how   This expression is wordy. Substitute *because.*

set – sit   *Set* means *to place; sit* means *to take a position.*

> Please set the package on the table.
>
> Please sit down and be quiet!

site   See *cite.*

slow – slowly   *Slow* and *slowly* both serve as adverbs. *Drive slow* and *Drive slowly* are equally acceptable.

so   *So* is often used as a conjunction expressing consequence, but it is often too weak for such a function. Instead of saying:

> The Committee has worked hard to prepare this report, so we hope that you will read it very carefully.

it would have been better to say:

> Since the Committee has worked hard to prepare this report, we hope that you will read it very carefully.

or

> The Committee has worked hard to prepare this report; therefore, we hope that you will read it very carefully.

In fact, it is a good idea to use *so* only when coupled with *that*.

> Andrew is so skilled an athlete that we all admire him.

somewheres　*Somewheres* is unacceptable. Say *somewhere*.

sooner　Say *sooner . . . than*, not *sooner . . . when*.

> No sooner had I mailed the letter than [not *when*] I realized that I had attached no postage.

sort(s)　See *kind(s)*.

sort of　See *kind of*.

sporadic　See *erratic*.

stationary – stationery　*Stationary* means at rest. *Stationery* refers to writing equipment.

> The missile is not stationary.

> Your stationery is elegant.

superior to　*Superior to* is the appropriate idiom, not *superior than*.

supposed to　Keep the final *-d* in *supposed* even though it is often not audible in pronunciation.

take　See *bring*.

that

a) Demonstrative pronoun or adjective: *that girl*. Its use as a pronoun should be avoided unless the antecedent is absolutely clear.

> The colonists were demanding representation and were insisting upon governing themselves. That gradually led to a confrontation between the old world and the new.

The *that* should have been *that spirit* or *that tension* or an equivalent.

b) Introduces a noun clause: I read that . . .
　　　　　　　　　　　　　　　　I heard that . . .

[Don't say: *I read where . . .*]

c) Used after a word of doubting.

I don't doubt that [not *but that*] there may be some truth to what you're saying.

d) A relative pronoun used to introduce an essential clause — as opposed to *which*, a pronoun used to introduce unessential clauses.

The commander would hear no idea that contradicted his beliefs.

e) When *that* introduces a single clause, don't repeat it, even after a long interruption.

It is hard to believe *that* in our advanced world today, with all man's extensive knowledge, *that* brutality still exists.

One of those two *that's* should be deleted.

f) However, *that* should be repeated when it introduces more than one clause.

I hope that they will arive soon and *that* they will be comfortable.

their – there – they're   *Their* = possessive: *of them. They're* = a contraction for *they are. There* is a demonstrative adverb indicating position or place.

over there   there are several reasons

theirselves   *Theirselves* is unacceptable. Use *themselves.*

them   *Them* as a demonstrative adjective *(them people)* is unacceptable. Use *these* or *those.*

theory   See *hypothesis.*

thusly   This word has not been recognized as acceptable. Use *thus.*

try   *Try* should be followed by an infinitive, not by *and.*

CORRECT: Try to concentrate.

INCORRECT: Try and concentrate.

uninterested   See *disinterested.*

used to   Keep the *-d* in *used* even though it is frequently not sounded in pronunciation.

wake   See *awake.*

well   *Well* is usually an adverb: *She sang well.* However, after a linking verb (such as *be, seem, look, appear, feel*), *well* is an adjective referring to good health.

The plan looks good.   [not referring to good health]

You look well today.   [referring to health]

You look good in your uniform.   [not referring to health]

when   Say *occurs when,* not *is when.*

True faith occurs when questions no longer have to be asked.

True faith is no longer having to ask questions.

where This word refers to location. It should not be used to introduce a statement.

INCORRECT: I read where Cleveland is in serious financial trouble.

CORRECT: I read that Cleveland is in serious financial trouble.

INCORRECT: Mitosis is where a cell divides exactly in half.

CORRECT: Mitosis occurs when a cell divides exactly in half.

CORRECT: Mitosis is the process by which a cell divides exactly in half.

whether Use *whether,* not *if* or *that* or *as,* to introduce a statement that expresses an alternative — that is, one in which the words *or not* are either stated or implied.

I'm not sure whether I know what you are talking about.

She asked me whether I would be able to drive her into town.

which *Which* as a relative pronoun introduces clauses that are not essential to the meaning of the sentence. When *which* appears as a relative pronoun, there should be a comma in front of it. *That,* on the other hand, introduces clauses that are essential to the meaning of a sentence. There is never a comma in front of *that* when it is being used as a relative pronoun.

Television, which is a relatively recent invention, has invaded the lives of almost every person in the country.

The television that you are watching has many unique features.

See Sections 4 K and 4 M.

whose – who's *Whose* = possessive: *of whom; who's* is a contraction for *who is; who'se* doesn't exist.

-wise Many people find this an offensive suffix: *I did well gradewise this term.* It would be wise to avoid it.

with See *at.*

your – you're *Your* = possessive: of you; *you're* is a contraction for *you are.*

38

Literary Terms

accent The stressed syllable of a word, such as the first syllable in *beau'ty*. Words of four or more syllables usually have at least two accents, the primary accent and the secondary accent(s). The main stress of the word is the primary accent; the less important stressed syllable or syllables form the secondary accents. The word *prestidigitation* has its primary accent on the fifth syllable and secondary accents on the first and third syllables: prés tĭ dí gĭ **tá** tĭon.

alexandrine A line of poetry with six iambic feet.

> Loving in truth, and fain in verse my love to show,
>
> That she, dear she, might take some pleasure of my pain

allegory A form of fiction in which specific characters and specific elements of plot and setting represent more universal aspects of life. A specific character may represent a type of person, a specific plot detail may represent a type of situation, and a specific place may represent a type of place. Examples: Orwell's *Animal Farm,* Bunyan's *Pilgrim's Progress,* Eudora Welty's "A Worn Path."

alliteration The repetition of consonant sounds at the beginning of words:

> *F*ifteen *f*earless *f*ighters *f*ought the *f*oe.

allusion A reference to some generally known body of knowledge, such as to Greek mythology, to the Bible, to a play of Shakespeare, to the bombing of Hiroshima, to a historical event.

ambiguity The presence of two or more possible meanings or interpretations to words or situations.

anachronism A person, object, or event that is placed in an inappropriate period of time. For instance, if a work of literature were set in ancient Rome and a person were to hear the tolling of a bell, that event would be anachronistic, since there were no bells in ancient Rome. Similarly, if a character in a contemporary story were to dress in the style of the 1920s and were to espouse attitudes of the 1920s, both that person's dress and the person's views might be considered anachronistic, and the person himself might be regarded as an anachronism.

anagnorisis A moment of revelation. A character finds out something about himself or herself that is painful and difficult to accept. The moment of anagnorisis is usually part of the climax and precedes the dénouement. It is a turning point in the action.

analogy A comparison of some of the specific similarities between two dissimilar objects—a human body, for instance, to an automobile engine. The adjective form is *analogous*.

anapest A pattern of rhythm consisting of two unstressed syllables followed by one stressed syllable, as in *ŭndĕrstánd*.

anaphora The repetition of words or phrases.

> Alone, alone, all, all alone,
> Alone on a wide wide sea.

antagonist The person in conflict with the main character.

anthropomorphism The assigning of human qualities to nonhuman creatures or to objects. The Greek gods, for instance, are said to be anthropomorphized because they are depicted in human form and have the same kinds of motivations that humans have.

anticlimax A drop from the important to the unimportant or from the significant to the insignificant. An anticlimax is often a letdown: something important is expected to happen but it doesn't.

antistrophe See *classical tragedy*.

antithesis A pair of ideas or phrases that are grammatically balanced but that contrast each other: To err is human, to forgive divine.

aphorism A short statement that is moralistic or that makes some general observation about life or the world.

apostrophe A direct address to an idea or to an object or to a being that is not present.

> Milton, thou shoulds't be living at this hour.

archetype A specific event in history, literature, religion, mythology, or the like that is reenacted in or reset into a literary situation. For instance, the betrayal for money of a magnanimous leader by a follower might remind the reader of the archetypal betrayal of Christ by Judas.

aside A convention in drama in which a character makes a remark heard only by the audience. The remark indicates what is going on in the speaker's mind.

assonance The repetition of vowel sounds.

> And the misty sea seethed.

ballad A form of narrative poetry that highlights some dramatic event. The *folk ballad* is one that was originally sung; much of the action is developed through dialogue; it is short and uncomplex; more is implied than stated. The *literary ballad* is one that was consciously composed by a poet. It too is short and it too depicts a dramatic event, but it is often more subtle and sophisticated. A common form of stanza for the ballad is the four line stanza with a rhyme scheme of *a-b-c-b;* the first and third lines are often in iambic tetrameter and the second and fourth lines in iambic trimeter:

> There lived a wife at Usher's Well,
> And a wealthy wife was she;
> She had three stout and stalwart sons,
> And sent them o'er the sea.

bathos An unsuccessful attempt of a writer to be serious or emotional. The reader or audience laughs rather than cries. Bathos often results from overdone sentimentality.

blank verse A series of lines in unrhymed iambic pentameter.

cacophony The presence of harsh or unpleasant sounds.

caesura A place in a line of verse where the reader pauses. A major caesura occurs where there is a mark of punctuation. Minor caesuras occur between phrases. A major caesura is indicated by two parallel slanted lines, a minor caesura by one slanted line.

> There's a thief,//perhaps,//that listens/with a face/of frozen stone

characters The individuals in a work of fiction. A *flat, static,* or *one-dimensional* character is one who experiences no growth or change and is not fully developed. A *type* or *stock* character is one who represents a single type of personality trait. A *round, dynamic,* or *three-dimensional* character is one who is fully developed, who is complex, as we all are, and who is affected one way or another by the events of the narrative. A *foil* is a character who himself is unimportant in the narrative but through whom are revealed insights into other characters or who serves as a catalyst to other characters.

chorus A group of people in a drama who comment upon the events of the drama, often supply background information, and often represent conventional attitudes. The chorus is often a foil to the principal characters.

classical tragedy Dramatic works in ancient times were usually composed for religious festivals. There would usually be three tragedies – a trilogy – on a common theme, followed by a comedy. The following lists some of the features and conventions of the Greek tragedy:

a) The *plot* of a tragedy would have been familiar to the Greek audience; it usually derives from some mythological or historical event. What is important, therefore, is not the plot but the playwright's treatment of that plot.

b) The *action* often explores a person of significant stature (a member of the nobility, a king, a military leader) who espouses a certain position but who carries that position to extremes. The main character often commits *hubris* – that is, the character goes too far, will not listen to reason, goes to excess or threatens to take excessive measures to impose his or her will upon others. During the climax of the tragedy, the character experiences *anagnorisis,* a moment of truth or a revelation in which the character realizes that he or she has been wrong. The realization is usually too late, however; the character often destroys himself or herself, and some of the people close to the character are often either ruined or destroyed. Thus, the tragedy explores the disintegration and waste of an able individual.

c) The character often has a defect in his or her personality, a flaw or *hamartia,* that drives him or her to the act of hubris. This flaw is not a vice; it is a weakness. The flaw often manifests itself as an error in judgment.

d) There is a group of people called the *chorus* and a spokesman for them called the leader, or *choragoros.* The chorus usually reflects a conventional attitude; it tries to reason with the protagonist; it supplies background information; it comments on the events of the drama; and it often speaks in the most glaring platitudes.

e) Several times during the play there will be a *choral ode,* or *stasimon.* The language of these odes is flowery and often difficult to understand. The chorus sings and dances simultaneously. Its dance steps are first to the left, the *strophe;* then to the right, the *antistrophe.* The ideas expressed in these units are often balanced: the strophe expresses an idea and the antistrophe expresses an elaboration of that idea or a contrast to that idea.

f) The usual structure of the tragedy is as follows: (1) *Prologue:* the introduction; the major problem or issue of the play is identified. (2) *Parodos:* the chorus enters and comments upon the problem mentioned in the prologue. (3) A series of *episodes,* or scenes; a choral ode separates one scene from another. Here is where the action of the play is developed. (4) *Exodos:* the dénouement: all the events after the final choral ode; the aftermath of the tragic events.

g) There is very little physical action on stage. The action is developed through dialogue. There are often rapid exchanges of dialogue called *stichomythia.* Violent actions are not depicted. They are described, often by a messenger.

h) The actors are all male. When necessary, they play more than one role. They wear a mask to indicate a particular emotion, changing that mask when they want to convey a change of mood. The mask helps to amplify their voices. There are no more than three actors on stage at any one time. An actor who enters the stage from the right of the spectators is supposed to be coming from a city or harbor; an actor who enters from the left is supposed to be coming from the country.

i) The primary emphasis is upon speech, not upon gesture or movement.

j) The *unities (q.v.)* of time, place, and action are observed.

climax   The high point in a work of fiction.

comedy of humours   See *humor.*

comedy of manners   A type of dramatic comedy that ridicules human foibles. The characters are usually one-dimensional, representing certain human types: a miser, a hypochondriac, a misanthrope, a shrew, a fool, a pompous person, and so on.

comic relief   The insertion of a comic character or comic scene in order to relieve tension.

commedia dell'arte   A type of dramatic comedy popular in the sixteenth and seventeenth centuries. The actors would identify in advance the highlights of the plot, but their movements and lines on stage would be improvised.

comparison, devices of: See *simile, metaphor, analogy, allegory, symbol, allusion, archetype, conceit, fable, parable, extended metaphor, mixed metaphor.*

complication An event that disrupts the ordinary life of a character. A work of fiction often explores how a character responds to a complication.

conceit A highly intellectual, unusual, and extended comparison between two very dissimilar objects. An extended comparison between God and an elephant, for instance, might be a conceit. The point of the conceit is to discover some similarity in what had been previously considered dissimilar.

conflict A struggle or tension between two opposing elements or forces, such as a person vs. a person, a person vs. a group of people, a person vs. an aspect of nature, a person vs. an idea, an idea vs. an idea, one attitude vs. another attitude.

connotation The subjective association that a word may suggest. For instance, a snake may connote evil or treachery or temptation. A mountain may connote grandeur, independence, or isolation.

consonance The repetition of consonant sounds within words.
   With a thousand pains that vision's face was grained

contrast, devices of See *irony, oxymoron, paradox, anticlimax, understatement, antithesis.*

couplet Two lines of poetry that have end-rhyme and that serve as one unit of thought. The couplet is *closed* when the second line completes the thought:
   High from the chasms of chromatic sky,
   It thundered and bellowed with deafening cry.

The couplet is *open* when the thought continues beyond the two lines:
   When I some antique jar behold,
   Or white, or blue, or speck'd with gold,
   Vessels so pure, and so refined,
   Appear the types of woman-kind.

If the couplet is in iambic pentameter, it is called a *heroic couplet.*
   But past is all his fame. The very spot
   Where many a time he triumphed is forgot.

dactyl   A pattern of rhythm consisting of one stressed and two unstressed syllables, as in *párăllĕl.*

denotation   The literal, dictionary meaning of a word.

dénouement   The events that follow the climax in a work of fiction. The dénouement usually presents a resolution of the problems, a clarification of unexplained plot elements, and a relaxation of tension.

dental   A consonant sound produced when the tongue touches the upper front teeth, such as *d, t, th.*

deus ex machina   In ancient plays a dramatist would occasionally get a character out of a difficult situation by having a god swoop down and rescue that character. Nowadays, when a farfetched means – often a coincidence – is employed to get a character out of a ticklish situation, that means is referred to as a *deus ex machina.*

diction   In literature, the type of words being used – fancy, intellectual, simple, vulgar, colloquial, bombastic, euphonous, harsh, mellow, long, short, and so on.

didactic   Literature written to teach. It is often moralistic.

dimeter   A line of verse that has two metrical feet.

> When the tyrant
> Saw the rebel

double rhyme   See *feminine rhyme.*

dramatic monologue   A type of poem in which a speaker soliloquizes. The act of soliloquizing is tantamount to an act of thinking. Hence, as the person speaks, he reveals his inner thoughts. As he reveals his thoughts, he reveals a great deal about himself – more than he realizes – and the reader gains insights that the speaker himself does not have. The dramatic monologue usually contains much dramatic irony.

dramatic poetry   Poetry whose primary purpose is to reveal the character of a person rather than to tell a story or to create a mood or to explore an idea or an emotion.

elegy   A type of poetry that laments someone or something that is no longer present. It often deals with death, and it is often a catalyst for the speaker of the poem to become introspective.

elision   The dropping of a vowel at the end of a word when the next word begins with a vowel: *th' empyreal sky;* or the dropping of a syllable within a word: *whate'er* for *whatever.*

ellipsis The omission of a word or of words. The reader or listener is expected to supply the missing word(s). For instance, the expression *Good morning!* is elliptical; the expression actually means "I wish you a good morning" or some such equivalent. The following interchange from Shakespeare's *Coriolanus* illustrates ellipses; the elliptical material is in parentheses:

"Would you proceed especially against Caius Marcius?"

"(I would proceed) Against him first; he's a very dog to the commonality."

"Consider you what services he has done for his country?"

"(I consider them) Very well, and (I) could be content to give him good report for't but that he pays himself with being proud."

end-rhyme The rhyming of final syllables at the end of lines of poetry. See *masculine rhyme, feminine rhyme, triple rhyme, half rhyme, false rhyme, pararhyme.*

end-stopped A line of verse that has a pause or a caesura at the end of the line. There is usually a punctuation mark at the end of the line.

English sonnet See *sonnet.*

enjambment A direct continuation of thought from one line of verse to the next line. The reader cannot pause at the end of the line but must continue to read in order to complete the thought.

And nobody could enough admire
The tall man and his quaint attire.

Another name for enjambment is *run-on line.*

epic A long poem, usually divided into subsections called *books* or *cantos.* The epic deals with the exploits, trials, tribulations, and triumphs of a hero, who often himself symbolically represents a particular culture and its political, national, ethical, cultural, or religious ideals. The *primary epic,* or *folk epic,* is one like the *Iliad, Odyssey, Beowulf,* or *Gilgamesh* that was not consciously composed by any one person at any one time but rather that evolved over a long period of time, usually through the oral tradition of wandering singers and storytellers. The *secondary epic,* or *literary epic,* is one like the *Aeneid, Divine Comedy,* or *Paradise Lost* that was actually consciously composed by a single person. The secondary epic is often more introspective, more self-conscious, and more concerned with style and elegance of expression than the primary epic is. While the epic poem is serious and lofty, the *mock epic* is satiric. The mock epic uses many of the conventions of the epic — extended similes, ostensibly serious topics, mythological and historical allusions, dignified language and tone — for comic effect. In the mock epic, there is often much fuss over nothing: triviality becomes magnified. The poet, instead of admiring and respecting his characters, laughs at them for their pretentiousness and foolishness. Pope's *Rape of the Lock* and Byron's *Don Juan* are splendid mock epics. Sometimes the word *epic* is applied loosely to a novel or a movie, such as *Gone with the Wind* or *Atlas Shrugged;* in this context, the word is usually synonymous with *monumental* or *impressive* or *very long.*

epigram A short, concise, and often witty statement. The epigram often appears in verse form, most commonly in heroic couplets:

A little learning is a dang'rous thing:
Drink deep, or taste not the Pierian spring.

The epigram often employs an antithesis — for example, Shaw's "The more things a man is ashamed of, the more respectable he is" — or a turn of the language — for example, Wilde's "The only way to get rid of a temptation is to yield to it."

epitaph An inscription on a tombstone, usually identifying and commemorating the deceased.

epithet An adjective closely associated with a particular noun, such as the *rosy-fingered* dawn; the *wily* Odysseus; the *big, bad* wolf. See also *transferred epithet.*

euphemism The expressing of an unpleasant idea with words of more pleasant or more elevated connotations; an attempt to sugarcoat something unpleasant or unattractive; an attempt to remove or to tone down the pejorative connotations of a word or an idea, such as *steeped in wine* for *drunk* or *passed away* for *died.*

euphony The presence of pleasant, attractive, or gentle sounds.

exaggeration and **toning down,** devices of See *hyperbole, understatement, euphemism, anticlimax, litotes.*

exposition The exposition in a work of fiction presents the major characters, the conflicts, the ideas, and the other essential elements that are later to be developed.

extended metaphor   A metaphor that is fully and elaborately developed. If the comparison is highly intellectual or unorthodox, the extended metaphor may be a conceit.

eye rhyme   See *false rhyme.*

fable   A short narrative, often with animals as the main characters, intended to illustrate a moral. The moral is usually about some common-sense aspect of life.

false rhyme   Syllables that have similar letters but dissimilar sounds and are put at the end of lines of verse to give the appearance of rhyme.

> In behalf of all that's good,
> Let us thank God for this food,
> Earned with toil and honest blood.

False rhyme is sometimes called *eye rhyme, sight rhyme,* or *slant rhyme.*

feminine ending   An extra unaccented syllable at the end of a line of verse.

Ănd ĭf| I hád| ă chánce| tŏ líve| ă nó|blĕ

feminine rhyme   The rhyming of the final two syllables in lines of verse. The final syllable of each line is usually unaccented, such as the rhyming of *sighting* and *fighting.* Feminine rhyme is sometimes called *double rhyme.*

figurative language   The use of words to express more than just the denotative meaning. Figurative language is suggestive; it tries to involve the reader and to stimulate his imagination and his senses.

figure of sound   See *sound, figure of.*

figure of speech   See *speech, figure of.*

flashback   The presentation of an event that happened before the events currently occurring.

flat character   See *characters.*

foil   See *characters.*

foot   A unit of rhythm. There are five common types of feet:

the iamb: *bĕliéve*   the trochee: *énter*
the dactyl: *túrpĕntīne*   the anapest: *ĭntĕrfére*
the spondee: *bâsebāll*

The progression of feet in verse determines the meter. Hence, if a series of lines of a verse each have five feet and the dominant type of foot is the dactyl, the meter of the verse is described as dactylic pentameter.

foreshadowing   The suggesting or hinting of an event that will occur later.

free verse   Lines of verse that have no fixed type of metrical foot, no fixed number of metrical feet in a line, and no fixed rhyme scheme.

gothic novel   A style of novel that revels in the supernatural, the macabre, and the ghoulish. Bram Stoker's *Dracula* and Mary Shelley's *Frankenstein* are two of the most famous gothic novels; Matthew Lewis' *The Monk* is perhaps the most spectacular.

guttural   A consonant sound produced in the throat, such as *k, q, x,* hard *c* (as in *cat*), hard *g* (as in *gun*). Gutturals are sometimes called *palatals.*

haiku   A verse form that originated in Japan; the haiku has three lines and a total of seventeen syllables. The first and the third line each have five syllables; the second line has seven syllables. The haiku consists of one statement in which the poet usually depicts an image.

half rhyme   A type of rhyme in which the vowels of final syllables of lines of verse rhyme but in which the consonants are different, such as *dance . . . pants* or *intellectual . . . henpecked you all.* Half rhyme is often used for humorous effect.

hamartia   See *classical tragedy.*

heptameter   A line of verse that contains seven metrical feet.

heroic couplet   Two lines of verse that express one unit of thought, are written in iambic pentameter, and contain end rhyme.

> Yes! let the rich deride, the proud disdain,
> These simple blessings of the lowly train.

hexameter   A line of verse that contains six metrical feet.

Homeric simile   A simile that is elaborately developed; it is sometimes called an *extended simile.*

> Just as when a traveler, worn from years of wandering and yearning to arrive home and once again see his dear wife and his aged parents and his children, finally setting his eyes upon his homeland, can scarcely hold back the tears, so did the weary Leontinus respond when he was reunited with his brother.

humor, or **humour** The late-Renaissance and the seventeenth-century mind at least half-seriously believed that one's disposition and temperament were dependent upon the dominance of a particular bodily fluid, or *humor*. There were four humors: a dominance of *blood* made one *sanguine* — cheerful, optimistic, robust, good-natured, extroverted, gregarious, and healthy; a dominance of *phlegm* made one *phlegmatic* — listless, inactive, diffident, lazy, and perhaps even stupid; *choler,* or *yellow bile,* made one *choleric* — cranky and irritable, stubborn, restless, and impatient; finally, *black bile* brought about *melancholy* — pensiveness, depression, moodiness, withdrawal, introspection. Eventually the concept of humors expanded to include any odd trait of human behavior; hence, there evolved the *comedy of humors:* plays in which characters were personifications or stereotypes of odd human traits, such as jealousy, greed, lust, naïveté, pompousness, stupidity, and so on. Ben Jonson's *Volpone* is a fine example of a comedy of humors.

hubris An act of excessiveness, of going too far, of forgetting or ignoring that one is human, not god. Hubris usually invites *nemesis:* when a character commits hubris, nemesis invariably follows. A person's nemesis is his downfall. *Hubris* is sometimes spelled *hybris*.

hyperbole Flagrant exaggeration: "I have a thousand things to do today."

iamb A pattern of rhythm consisting of one unaccented syllable followed by one accented syllable, as in *rĕpeát*.

imagery The phrasing of ideas in such a way as to stimulate the imagination and to appeal to the senses. Figures of speech and sound, comparisons, and figurative language contribute to the imagery of a work.

inciting action That particular event that initiates the conflict in a play or a narrative.

incremental repetition The repetition of phrases or of lines of verse that take on added significance with each new repetition. The repetition of the pattern "For I'm . . ., and fain would lie down" in the ballad "Lord Randall" is a good example.

internal rhyme The rhyming of syllables within a line of verse — as opposed to end rhyme.

I arise from dreams of thee
In the first sweet sleep of night

A type of internal rhyme is *leonine rhyme;* this occurs when a word within the line rhymes with the final syllable of the line:

With faces s*tern,* they tried to l*earn*

irony   Irony is a contrast. There are three types: *situational irony,* in which the opposite occurs from what one would expect; *dramatic,* or *Sophoclean irony,* in which the reader or audience knows information that a fictional character does not know and hence can often see the character doing things in his ignorance that will hurt him; *verbal irony* is an expression that means the opposite of what the words actually say.

Italian sonnet   See *sonnet.*

juxtaposition   The taking of two independent items—for example, facts, statements, paragraphs, scenes, stanzas—and looking at them together in order to draw an inference.

labial   A consonant pronounced with the lips, such as *p, b, ph, f, v.*

limerick   A narrative in verse form. A limerick has five lines and a total of thirteen metrical feet, usually anapests or iambs; the rhyme scheme is *a-a-b-b-a.* The limerick is usually used for humorous effect. A national limerick contest sponsored by Mohegan Community College in Connecticut in 1978 produced the following winner:

The bustard's an exquisite fowl
With minimal reason to growl:
    He escapes what would be
    Illegitimacy
By grace of a fortunate vowel.

liquid   A consonant that rolls or glides in the mouth, such as *l, m, n, r.*

litotes   A form of understatement in which an idea is expressed by negating the opposite of that idea: *not fat* for *skinny.*

lyric   The word has two senses. It can refer to song. Hence, when something is lyrical, it is songlike, suitable for singing; and, in fact, one talks about the *lyrics* of a song. *Lyric poetry,* on the other hand, is poetry whose intent is primarily to stimulate the imagination or to express a mood or a feeling rather than to tell a story or to portray a character.

malapropism   A word that is confused with a similar sounding word and hence that is misused: "He made a *receptacle* of himself" instead of "He made a *spectacle* of himself." Named after Mrs. Malaprop, a character noted for her misuse of words in R. B. Sheridan's comedy *The Rivals* (1775).

masculine ending A line of verse whose final syllable is accented.

> Whăt dángĕrs cánst thŏu máke ŭs scórn!

masculine rhyme A type of end rhyme in which only the last syllables rhyme, as in *stormy sea . . . company.*

metaphor A comparison which an author makes directly, without calling attention to it by using words such as *like* or *as*. An explicit metaphor is one like "England is a fen of stagnant waters." The pattern is *X is Y*. A more subtle metaphor is one like "We must weed out the traitors." *Weed out* is not to be taken literally—in fact, a metaphor is usually foolish if taken literally; rather the metaphor compares the literal act of removing traitors to the act of removing weeds: the undesirable is removed from the desirable.

meter The progression of rhythm. It is the progression of units of stressed and unstressed syllables—that is, of feet. To identify the meter of lines of verse, one identifies the dominant type of foot and the prevalent number of feet in each line, such as dactylic hexameter, iambic pentameter, trochaic trimeter.

metonymy Using a word closely connected with another word instead of that other word: "We approached the *bench*" instead of "We approached the judge." The *Oval Office* instead of the *President.*

microcosm A miniature representation or restatement of an issue, conflict, or theme. Often a subplot in a novel or a seemingly irrelevant detail in a short story contains in microcosm one of the concerns of that novel or story.

mixed metaphor A comparison that begins comparing X to Y and ends up comparing X to Z. For example: "Her *acid* tongue and *caustic* wit *drowned* all opposition." The comparison begins by comparing her remarks to something that burns and ends by comparing her remarks to something that overflows. The metaphor can be unified by making consistent all the terms of comparison: "Her burning tongue and caustic wit *scorched* all opposition."

mock epic See *epic.*

monometer   A line of verse with only one metrical foot.

morality play or **morality tale**   A work of fiction in which the characters tend to stand for qualities or abstractions and in which the plot tends to be allegorical and often religious. Rather than being fully developed and complex human beings, the characters tend to be types and are usually one-dimensional. The most common themes are the conflict between good and evil, man's voyage on the path of life, and the dangers and allurements of vice. Many works of literature are in the tradition of the morality play or morality tale. Shakespeare's *Winter's Tale,* for instance, although it is not overtly religious, has many of the trappings of a morality play: the essential conflict is between good and evil; the play explores the destructiveness of a particular type of evil (jealousy) and it shows the redemptive qualities of love and trust. The characters tend to personify qualities: patience and strength (Hermione); loyalty (Camillo); conscience (Paulina); innate goodness and nobility (Perdita); jealousy (Leontes); pure love (Florizel); knavery (Autolycus); and so on.

motif   A recurrent idea, detail, or pattern. A motif can occur in any of the arts: music, literature, painting, architecture, sculpture, dance, design, and so on.

motivation   That which prompts a person to respond or to react or to behave in the way that he does.

muses   Nine sisters, goddesses of inspiration: Calliope, the Muse of epic poetry; Clio, the Muse of history; Euterpe, the Muse of lyric poetry and flute playing; Thalia, the Muse of comedy; Melpomene, the Muse of tragedy; Terpsichore, the Muse of the dance; Erato, the Muse of love and erotic poetry; Polyhymnia, the Muse of lofty and sacred poetry and hymns; and Urania, the Muse of astronomy.

narrative poem   A poem whose primary intent is to tell a story rather than to depict character or to explore feelings, ideas, emotions, moods or to present images.

nasal   A sound that is pronounced through the nose, such as *n, ng,* and sometimes *m.*

octameter   A line of verse that has eight metrical feet.

octave   A unit of eight lines of verse. The octave can stand alone as a stanza or it can serve as one of the structural units of a sonnet. See *sonnet.*

ode An extended, sophisticated, and often complex lyric poem in which a poet explores his thoughts and feelings about and his reactions to a person or thing or event. That person or thing or event to which the ode is directed is often just a catalyst for the poet to become introspective.

omniscient narrator See *point of view.*

onomatopoeia The recreation of sounds into words: *whoosh, splash, buzz.* The word attempts to echo the sound.

ottava rima A stanza with eight lines and a rhyme scheme of *a-b-a-b-a-b-c-c.*

oxymoron A phrase that contains two words, each contradicting the other:

happy sadness   *roaring silence*   *she spoke silently*

paean A hymn of praise, joy, thanksgiving, victory, etc.

paeon A foot with three unstressed and one stressed syllables:

Whén Ĭ hĕard thĕ| béck'nĭng ŏf thĕ| sólĭtărў| séa

parable A short narrative intended to teach a lesson or to offer a moral. It differs from the fable by not having animals as principal characters and by having morals that are more philosophic or spiritual than those of the fable; the parable is also more serious than the fable.

paradox A statement that seems to contradict itself, such as *Only through war can there ever be peace.*

paraphrase Taking a piece of writing and putting it into your own words. The paraphrase aims to clarify and explain; it tries to remove ambiguities and to clarify obscurities; it changes metaphors into similes; it explains allusions. It alters the words of the original but never the thought or the meaning.

pararhyme The rhyming of consonants instead of vowels; similar consonants surround different vowels:

hair . . . hour   *spoiled . . . spilled*   *killed . . . cold*
war . . . were

parody A piece of prose or verse that imitates some other piece of prose or verse and, in the process of imitating, ridicules the original.

pastoral A type of literature that extols the country and the rustic type of life. The setting is often *Arcadia,* or *Arcady,* although it can be anywhere – even Bohemia, as in Act IV of Shakespeare's *Winter's Tale*. The rustic life is idealized; it is depicted as pure and uncorrupted, almost utopian, a place where the passions are absent and where there is no real vice. Life is idyllic. It is a world where shepherds and shepherdesses tend to their sheep, live a simple and unsophisticated life, enjoy themselves in festivals, songs, and dances; there is much fellowship; it is a gregarious world where almost everyone is friendly with everyone else. Music and flowers are everywhere. People live a life of peace, simplicity, and contentment. The shepherdesses are often named Phyllis or Amaryllis, Chloe, Sylvia, Clora or Clorinda, Flora, Celia, or Cynthia.

pathetic fallacy Attributing human reactions and emotions to objects.

> When the death of the king was announced, even the trees moaned throughout the forest.

The people's reaction is projected upon the trees. The pathetic fallacy is a type of personification.

pathos Genuine and sincere appeal to the emotions, especially the emotions of pity, concern, sorrow, and sympathy. When the motivation for this appeal is insincere and contrived, the pathos often becomes *melodrama*. And when the emotional appeal is excessive and unbelievable, the pathos becomes *bathos:* one laughs instead of cries.

pentameter A line of verse that has five metrical feet.

periodic sentence The strict definition of a periodic sentence is a complex sentence that has its main clause at the end of the sentence; therefore, one must wait for the end in order for the sentence to be complete. The term is usually used more loosely to refer to complex sentences in general, often to elegant, carefully crafted, and sometimes quite involved sentences.

persona Literally, a mask. When a writer wishes to make a point, he sometimes creates a speaker or a character who espouses a point of view totally opposite to the point that the author espouses. As the speaker or character presents his ideas, he reveals himself to be a fool. Hence, the author, by masking his own feelings, has exposed the folly of his opposition. The arguments of a persona are an example of extended verbal irony. The speaker of Jonathan Swift's "A Modest Proposal" is a fine example of a persona.

personification The treatment of animals or objects as if they were living human beings; they are given a human personality and human emotions. The apostrophe and the pathetic fallacy are types of personification; anthropomorphism is also a type of personification.

Petrarchan sonnet See *sonnet.*

picaresque A type of novel or story that traces the life and adventures of a rogue, or *picaro.* The hero is usually a vagabond who goes through a series of comic adventures and is often a trickster. *Huck Finn* and *Tom Jones* are good examples of picaresque novels. The picaresque novel often contains comic social commentary, for the *picaro's* meanderings put him in contact with people of different social classes, and the novel often treats these people satirically.

pleonasm A redundancy: *she saw with her eyes; he returned back to his home.*

plosive A consonant that requires a brief explosion of air, such as a *b,* hard *c* (as in *cough*), *d, f,* hard *g* (as in *gas*), *k, p, q, t, x.*

poetic justice When the bad guys get the punishment they deserve and the good guys get the reward they deserve.

poetic license An author sometimes deviates from the conventions of grammar, sentence structure, word order, and the like. These transgressions are rationalized when we say that, being a writer or poet, he is above the ordinary conventions of writing – that is, that he has the poetic license to break the usual rules.

point of view The eyes through which the story is told. The story (or poem) always has a *speaker,* sometimes called a *narrator.* The speaker is not necessarily the same as the writer; in fact, he usually is not. The speaker is sometimes in the first person, sometimes merely telling the story, sometimes himself a participant in the action. Most of the time the speaker is in the third person. Sometimes he is an *omniscient narrator:* he has complete knowledge of the events; he can see all that is happening, and he selects from what he sees; he even knows what is going on in the mind of each character. A *limited omniscient* narrator is one who knows almost everything. To determine the point of view, explore these questions: Who is telling the story? How much does the narrator know? Is the narrator objective? Does he insert his own opinions or biases into the narrative? Does he display any attitude toward the various people or events that he is writing about, or is he maintaining a neutral attitude? Does he have any (ulterior) motive for telling the story? Picture the narrator. Picture his reactions as he is telling the story. Imagine the tone of voice he would use if he were telling the story orally.

preterition A rhetorical device in which the speaker says that he is not going to mention something at the very time that he is mentioning it:

> I will not say anything about the fact that your business associate mysteriously disappeared; I will not mention the many suspicions that surrounded his disappearance; nor will I say anything about your hostility to him. No, I shall remain silent on these matters.

protagonist The main character, whether villain or hero or just an ordinary, undistinguished person. The protagonist is not necessarily the good guy; the protagonist is merely the most important character.

quatrain A unit of four lines of verse. The quatrain can stand alone as a stanza or it can serve as one of the structural units of a sonnet. See *sonnet.*

quintain A unit of five lines of verse.

refrain A group of words, a line, or a series of lines that is repeated regularly throughout a piece of writing. The "Glory, glory, hallelujah" lines in "The Battle Hymn of the Republic" is an example.

repetition, figures of See *refrain, assonance, alliteration, consonance, anaphora, incremental repetition.*

rhetoric The art of writing or speaking effectively, eloquently, and persuasively. The word is sometimes loosely used to refer to eloquent but empty and insincere discourse.

rhetorical question A statement expressed as a question that expects no answer. The rhetorical question is posed more for effect and is, in fact, not really a question—for example, "Do you want to see your home go up in flames?" or "How are you?"

rhyme Words whose syllables have similar sounds, such as *ago . . . know . . . sew . . . foe . . . slow* or *hoot . . . root . . . brute . . . fruit.* See *end rhyme, masculine rhyme, feminine rhyme, triple rhyme, half rhyme, false rhyme, internal rhyme, pararhyme.*

rhyme royal A stanza of seven lines in iambic pentameter with the rhyme scheme a-b-a-b-b-c-c.

rhythm The pace, speed, or flow of a piece of writing. Do the words read quickly or slow? Do they read smoothly or choppily? Is there any pattern to the stressed and unstressed syllables? Is there any discernible meter? The rhythm often complements the action. Note, for instance, the speed of the following sentence from Dickens's *Tale of Two Cities:*

> The sound of a horse at a gallop came fast and furiously up the hill.

round character See *characters.*

run-on line See *enjambment.*

satire Any form of discourse that aims at ridiculing, exposing, and often poking fun at human folly or human nature. *Horatian satire* is gentle; it laughs with the people it is criticizing; it is disapproving but understanding. *Juvenalian satire,* on the other hand, is bitter; it laughs at those it is criticizing; it scorns, holds in contempt, and shows no mercy; it disapproves and condemns.

scansion The process of indicating the stressed and unstressed syllables in lines of poetry and of marking the metrical feet. The scansion for the following line is indicated:

Po͝or so͞ul,| thĕ cén|tĕr óf| my̆ sín|fŭl eárth

secondary accent See *accent.*

sestet A unit of six lines of verse. The sestet can stand alone as a stanza, or it can serve as one of the structural units of a sonnet. See *sonnet.*

setting All the elements that serve as a backdrop to a work of literature, such as the time, the broad geographical location (what country? in the city? suburbs? country? on sea?), the specific location, the arrangement of the physical items on stage, the weather, the mores of the characters.

Shakespearean sonnet See *sonnet.*

sibilant A consonant produced when air is driven between the tongue and the palate of the mouth, such as *s*, soft *c* (as in *cent*), and *z*.

sight rhyme See *false rhyme.*

simile A comparison introduced by words such as *like, just like, similar to.* Also see *Homeric simile.*

situation   The background events of a poem. Since a poem often explores just one moment of an event, the reader must often infer the larger context of that specific event. That larger context is the situation. To determine the situation, ask: "What has been happening up to the point when the poem begins?"

slant rhyme   See *false rhyme.*

soliloquy   A dramatic convention in which a person speaks alone. If there are other characters around him, they do not hear him. The soliloquy is tantamount to a character's thinking aloud: the audience can ascertain what is going on in the speaker's mind. See also *dramatic monologue.*

sonnet   A poem of fourteen lines, unified around one central idea, and invariably written in iambic pentameter. There are two conventional types of sonnets: the English or Shakespearean sonnet and the Italian or Petrarchan sonnet. The *English* sonnet divides into three quatrains and one couplet. Each of the three quatrains explores an idea from a slightly different perspective or in a slightly different way. The final couplet offers a conclusion or a resolution. The English sonnet is used by poets who want to analyze a situation or an idea or a problem. The *Italian* sonnet divides into an octave and a sestet. The octave presents or describes or defines a situation, idea, or problem, and the sestet offers the poet's reaction to that situation. The octave thus presents the problem and the sestet presents the resolution. The Italian form is used by poets who want to be more thorough in depicting and resolving a problem rather than in exploring the ramifications of that problem.

sound, figure of   An expression that calls attention to itself through the sounds of the words it uses. Examples are alliteration, assonance, consonance, onomatopoeia, and anaphora.

speech, figure of   An expression designed to call attention to itself either by the way it is phrased or by the unusual use of a word or of words. Examples are the simile, metaphor, personification, oxymoron, hyperbole.

Spenserian stanza   A stanza of nine lines with the rhyme scheme *a-b-a-b-b-c-b-c-c.* The first eight lines are in iambic pentameter; the final line is in iambic hexameter.

spondee   A unit or rhythm consisting of two heavy syllables, as in *bāsebāll* or *Shakespēāre.*

sprung rhythm A type of rhythm that regards only the number of stressed syllables in a line; any number of unstressed syllables may appear. The following line illustrates a pentameter in sprung rhythm:

Rún! | Rún frŏm thĕ | fóe! | Flée thĕ fĕ | rócĭŏus

sprung vowel A vowel that can be glided over in pronunciation, especially a vowel that comes before a liquid consonant; for instance, *gardening* can be pronounced as three syllables *gar-den-ing* or as two syllables *gar-dning; everett* can be pronounced *ev-er-ett* or *ev-rett*. The vowel can be sprung in or sprung out.

stanza A series of lines of verse that serve as a single unit. The stanza is to the poem what the scene is to a play or what a chapter is to a novel.

stock characters See *characters.*

stream-of-consciousness A type of writing that tries to reproduce or imitate the thought process. Image follows image, seemingly without connection. The writing seems incoherent and rambling, disorganized, disjointed. Stream-of-consciousness writing reflects some of the findings of modern psychiatry, particularly those findings having to do with the free associations of ideas and images and with word association.

strophe See *classical tragedy.*

structure The units of thought that comprise a work of fiction. When one examines the structure, one notes the way the events or the scenes have been arranged, how thoroughly they have been treated, and how each contributes to the work as a whole.

subplot A scene or a sequence of events that is not directly related to the main plot. The subplot often offers a different perspective to some idea that the main plot is developing.

substitution The insertion of a metrical foot different from the dominant type of metrical foot in a poem. For instance, if the dominant type of foot were the iamb, a substitution would occur if one of the iambs were replaced by a dactyl, a trochee, or an anapest.

symbol An object or a detail whose importance lies in what that object or detail represents rather than in the actual object or detail *per se.* A balloon, for instance, might symbolize a type of life with a highly fragile but deceptively flexible exterior. The inflating of the balloon might be used to suggest increased pressures on a person. The bursting of the balloon might suggest frustrated aspirations or it might suggest that the pressures have become too great. The interpretation of a symbol is invariably subjective, and there are usually several possible interpretations.

synaesthesia Describing one sensuous phenomenon with words that usually apply to a different sense, such as describing sound in terms of color: *her black tones;* or objects in terms of sound: *in some melodious plot of beachen green.*

synecdoche Using a part of something to refer to the whole: *prows* or *masts* for *ships,* for instance, or *spires* for *churches.*

syntax The grammatical relationship of a word to the sentence it is in. It is especially important to observe the syntax of words in poetry because of the often unconventional word order. For instance, the following lines from Shelley's "Ozymandias" are baffling unless one determines the syntax of the word *hand.* (It is the direct object of *survive.*)

> Half sunk, a shattered visage lies, whose frown,
> And wrinkled lip, and sneer of cold command,
> Tell that its sculptor well those passions read
> Which yet survive, stamped on these lifeless things,
> The hand that mocked them, and the heart that fed.

tercet A unit of three lines of verse.

terza rima A verse form of three-line stanzas, written in iambs, and usually in pentameter, with the rhyme scheme of *a-b-a, b-c-b, c-d-c, d-e-d, e-f-e, etc.*

tetrameter A line of verse with four metrical feet.

theme The central idea suggested by a work of literature. The plot is literal and refers to the specific events; the theme is more universal. The theme is a general statement about some aspect of life, human behavior, or human personalities.

transferred epithet An adjective that inappropriately or illogically modifies a noun. In the sentence

> The sailors, finally rescued from the waves, steered a relieved course homeward.

the adjective *relieved* is a transferred epithet: the course was not relieved; the sailors were relieved. The position of the adjective has been transferred for emphasis.

trimeter A line of verse with three metrical feet.

triple rhyme The rhyming of the last three syllables in lines of verse:

> notorious . . . victorious   sanity . . . vanity
> dust arise . . . must comprise.

trochee   A metrical foot consisting of one stressed syllable followed by an unstressed syllable, as in *únděr.*

trope   Another name for *figure of speech.*

type characters   See *characters.*

understatement   Saying something with less intensity than is possible; depicting something as less than it is.

unities   The unities were a convention of the classical theater. The *unity of time* required that the plot of a play be confined to a twenty-four-hour period. The *unity of place* required that there be only one setting. The *unity of action* required that there be no subplots but rather that the play develop only one line of action.

variation   A break in pattern. If a series of lines have been in tetrameter and a line suddenly appears in pentameter, that odd line is a variation. If a series of stanzas contain eight lines and suddenly a stanza appears with six lines, that odd stanza is a variation. Since a variation is a noticeable break in pattern, it is important to account for variations in a piece of literature.

vignette   A short, self-contained scene in a work of fiction.

willing suspension of disbelief   There are times when a work of fiction depicts an impossible series of events. If, however, the reader is willing to accept as possible one of these impossibilities, the rest of the work makes good sense. For instance, Orwell's *Animal Farm* has animals talking. This is clearly impossible. But if the reader is willing to allow Orwell this one liberty — that is, if the reader is willing to suspend his disbelief in this one phenomenon — the rest of the story makes perfect sense.

zeugma   A zeugma occurs when a word governs at least two other words but when at least one of those other words is inappropriate. The most common type of zeugma occurs when a verb takes two different objects, only one of which is appropriate.

> Here thou, great Anna! whom three realms obey,
> Dost sometimes counsel take — and sometimes Tea.

The zeugma is often used for humorous effect. When it is used inadvertently, grammatical problems such as those described in Section 11 G result.

39

Abbreviations and Foreign Words

The citation of abbreviations varies from publication to publication. For instance, the abbreviation for *afternoon (post meridiem)* can be written P.M., PM, p.m., pm. There is also variation in the italicizing of foreign words and their abbreviations. The usual guideline is not to italicize foreign expressions that have become incorporated into the English language, but people will differ in what they feel has become truly incorporated and what should be regarded as foreign.

ad lib. *(ad libitum)*   As you wish.

Ae./ae./aet./aetat. *(aetatis)*   At the age of.

ante   Before.

ar/ar./arr/arr.   Arrival; arranged (by).

ca. *(circa)*   Around, approximately.
Born *ca.* 1800.

cf. *(confer)*   Compare.

c/o   (in) care of.

cp.   Compare.

do/do.   Ditto, the same.
Beethoven, Pathétique Sonata: $1.50.
do., simplified edition: $1.25.

e.g. *(exempli gratia)*   For example.
Several composers – e.g., Beethoven, Schumann, Schubert – never lived to hear many of their works performed.

est.   1) Estimated.   2) Established.

ETA/E.T.A.   Estimated time of arrival.

et al. (et alii, et alia)   And others.

etc. *(et cetera)*   And the rest, and so forth.
A comma precedes the abbreviation and, if the sentence continues, a comma follows the abbreviation.

et seq. (et sequens)   And the following; and what comes after.

ff.   Following.
> See page 65 ff. = See page 65 and the pages that follow it.

fl. *(floruit)*   He/she flourished; he/she produced his/her most significant work. Often used of people whose exact dates are uncertain.

HMS/H.M.S.   His/Her Majesty's Ship.
> HMS *Pinafore.*

ib./ibid. (ibidem)   The same. In footnotes *ibid.* refers to the same source as indicated in the previous footnote.

id./idem   The same. This abbreviation has recently yielded to *ibid.*

i.e. *(id est)*   That is to say, namely.
> Those diseases – i.e., mononucleosis and mumps – are particularly contagious.

infra   Below.

l./ll.   Line/lines. Usually used to refer to lines of poetry.

loc. cit. (loco citato)   In the place already cited. This abbreviation used to be used in footnotes but has recently been replaced by *ibid.,* or by the author's last name followed by the first words of the title.

m.d. *(manu dextra)*   With the right hand.

Messrs.   The plural of Mr.
> Messrs. Landau, Linn, and Briger will represent us at the conference.

Mlle(s).   Mademoiselle(s).

Mme(s).   Madame, Mesdames.

mo.   Month.

MS/M.S./ms.   Manuscript. Add *-s* for plural: MSS/mss.

m.s. *(manu sinistra)*   With the left hand.

N.B. *(nota bene)*   Note well! Pay close attention!

n.d.   No date. Used in footnotes and bibliographies to indicate that the date of publication is not available.

no(s).   Number(s).

né   Born with the name of. Refers to the original name of a male who is now using a different name.

née   Feminine form of *né*.
Madame Bovary, *née* Rouault.

non seq. *(non sequitur)*   It does not follow. Used of a statement that has no logical connection with or relevance to the previous statement.

NT   The New Testament.

ob. *(obiit)*   He/she died.

Op./op. *(opus)*   A (published) work, usually a piece of music.
Brahms's Quintet, Op. 34.

op. cit. *(opere citato)*   In the work cited. Used in footnotes to refer to a particular title recently mentioned in the footnotes.

OT   The Old Testament.

passim   Here and there. If an index to a book uses *passim* instead of giving specific page references, there are probably too many references to be catalogued; the reader should expect to find references on almost any page he turns.

p./pp.   Page, pages.
See pp. 26 – 35 = See pages 26 through 35.

post   After.

PTO   Please turn over. Indicates that the reader should turn the page.

QED *(quod erat demonstrandum)*   That which we set out to prove. Indicates that the proof has been completed.

Q.T./QT *(quod tacendum)*   This must be kept quiet. If you hear something *on the Q.T.*, you hear it in confidence.

q.v. *(quod vide)*   Refer to it.
Mars: Roman equivalent to Ares *(q.v.)*. The abbreviation suggests that the reader consult *Ares* for further references.

re   In regard to, concerning. Sometimes one will see *in re*.

RSVP *(Répondez s'il vous plaît)*   Please reply.

rte./rte Route.

sc./scil. *(scilicet)* Namely, that is to say.

seq(q). *(sequens, sequentia)* The following. Often refers to a sequel.

sic Thus. Indicates that the writer has purposely written or spelled something in a particular way; it often indicates that the writer is reproducing something exactly from the original, even if that original contained an error.

stat *(statim)* Immediately.

stet Let it stand. When one indicates a deletion or correction in one's text and then realizes that that deletion or correction is unwarranted, *stet* indicates that the original should be kept and that the correction or deletion should be ignored.

supra Above.

v./vid. *(vide)* See. The abbreviation asks the reader to look elsewhere in the text, probably for a cross reference.

viz. *(videlicet)* Namely.

vs. Versus.

40

Grammatical Terms

For terms used in this book that do not appear in this glossary, please consult the index.

absolute phrase   See *participle.*

accusative case   Equivalent to the objective case in English.

active voice   See the discussion of *voice,* Chapter 11.

adjective   See Chapter 8.

adjective clause   See *clause.*

adverb   See Chapter 8.

adverbial clause   See *clause.*

agreement   See Chapters 3 and 4. Agreement refers to the consistent presentation of two or more items that function together, such as subject and verb, pronoun and antecedent, adjective and noun.

a) A subject and its verb must agree in person and number:

the girl is	the girls are	I am	she goes
the girl was	the girls were	we are	they go

b) A pronoun and its antecedent agree in person and number and gender:

the man . . . he   the men . . . they   the girl . . . she
the girls . . . they   the house . . . it
the boy . . . who is coming   the car that we bought

c) An adjective and the word it describes agree in number:

this person   those people   that is the type
those are the types

antecedent   The word(s) that a pronoun stands for.

Diana is my sister. Do you know her?

Her stands for *Diana;* therefore, the antecedent of *her* is *Diana.*

Brian and Terry, whom we visited last weekend, . . .

Whom stands for *Brian* and *Terry;* therefore, the antecedent of *whom* is *Brian* and *Terry.*

The criminals outfoxed themselves.

Themselves stands for *criminals;* therefore, the antecedent of *themselves* is *criminals.*

appositive   A word or group of words that precisely identifies or renames a noun or pronoun. If the appositive is essential to the meaning of a sentence, it is not set off by commas. If it is not essential to the meaning of a sentence but if it merely adds additional information, then it is set off by commas.

Tolstoy's novel *War and Peace* is magnificent.

Tolstoy's longest novel, *War and Peace,* is magnificent.

The appositive in each sentence is *War and Peace.* Commas are not used in the first sentence because the reader cannot be sure exactly what novel is being referred to; hence the appositive is essential to the meaning of the sentence. In the second example, however, there can be only one long*est* novel; therefore, the appositive is merely adding helpful but unessential information.

Francis and William, both characters of the highest order, will be traveling together this summer.

The words set off by commas are an appositive phrase adding additional but unessential information about Francis and William.

article   *A, an, the. A* and *an* are indefinite articles; *the* is a definite article.

auxiliary   A word that indicates the mood, tense, voice, number, or aspect of a verb.

I *am* going   we *were being* seen   I *may be* visited
they *will have been* gone   you *might have* asked

cardinal numeral   See *numeral.*

case   The grammatical relationship of a noun, pronoun, or adjective to the sentence in which it appears. See Chapter 6.

a) Subject (nominative) case:

They have already arrived.

Can *we* offer you any assistance?

May *I* leave now.

b) Possessive case:

This is *mine.*

This is *Ramsey's.*

The reward is *yours.*

c) Object(ive) case:

We have not yet seen *them.*

Can you help *me?*

I left *her* an hour ago.

clause   A group of words that has a subject and a complete verb. A *main,* or *independent* clause is one that stands alone as a complete sentence, for it expresses a complete thought.

Joseph Glidden invented barbed wire in 1874.

A *subordinate,* or *dependent* clause cannot stand alone as a sentence, for it does not express a complete thought:

when Joseph Glidden invented barbed wire in 1874

A *complex sentence* is a sentence that contains one main clause and at least one subordinate clause.

Joseph Glidden, who was born in Charlestown, New Hampshire, invented barbed wire in 1874.

If the main clause is missing, one has a *sentence fragment.* (See Sections 2 E and 16 F.)

Types of dependent clauses

An *essential,* or *restrictive* clause is one that is necessary to the meaning of the sentence. The meaning of the sentence would be distorted if the clause were removed.

People *who lie* are not to be trusted.

Babies *that incessantly cry* are nuisances.

An *unessential,* or *nonrestrictive* clause is one that is not necessary to the meaning of the sentence. The clause could be removed without altering the meaning of the sentence.

Barbed wire, which was invented in 1874, was used before the discovery of the electrified fence.

An *adjective clause* is one that describes a noun or a pronoun. It is introduced by a relative pronoun: *who, whom, whose, which, that.* The adjective clause is set off by commas when it is not essential to the meaning of the sentence:

The city of Petrograd, which had been founded in 1703 and called St. Petersburg, was renamed Leningrad.

Mr. Todd, who heads the antismoking campaign, used to be a heavy smoker.

The adjective clause is not set off by commas when it is essential to the meaning of the sentence.

no comma
↓

Oman, a country *that was relatively poor two decades ago,* is now relatively prosperous because of its newly found oil.

no comma   no comma
↓   ↓

A person *who heads the antismoking campaign* must be a nonsmoker.

no comma
↓

I avoid people *whose comments are consistently caustic.*

An *adverbial clause* is one that modifies a verb or occasionally an adjective or another adverb. It answers the question *why?* or *where?* or *when?* or *how?* or to what *extent?*

When?   *After the storm was over,* Philip and Mark went sailing.
While elections are being held, there must be no campaigning.

Why?   Daniyal went to Pakistan *so that he might visit his family.*
Because you have lied to me, I can no longer trust you.

To what extent?   John is more interested in photography *than I am.*
The leader was so powerful *that everyone feared him.*

Where?   They hid their treasure *where no one could find it.*

The adverbial clause is set off by commas when it appears at the beginning of a sentence or when it is within a sentence. It is usually not set off by commas when it ends the sentence.

Whenever there is a crisis, it seems that people quickly learn to work together.

It seems that, whenever there is a crisis, people quickly learn to work together.

It seems that people quickly learn to work together whenever there is a crisis.

A *noun clause* is a dependent clause used in the same way that a single noun is used. It is almost never set off by commas.

As a subject: *What I heard* amazed me.

As a direct object: Do you know *who has been invited?*
I believe *that all war is immoral.*

As a predicate nominative: The novel is *what I had expected.*

As an object of a preposition: Give it to *whoever claims it.*

collective noun   A noun that stands for a group of people, such as *committee, crew, team, group, crowd.* The collective noun is usually regarded as singular; however, if the noun wants to stress the diversity among the members of the group, then it is regarded as plural.

comparative degree   Used when referring to adjectives and adverbs. See Chapter 9, Sections A and B.

complement   A word or group of words used to complete the meaning of a verb.

Predicate noun: We are *diplomats.*

Predicate adjective: We are *fearless.*

Direct object: We visited the *diplomats.*

Indirect object: We gave the *diplomats* the message.

Objective complement: We made her *chairman.*

complex sentence   See Chapter 2 D.

compound   When two or more equal elements are joined by a conjunction, those elements are said to be compounded.

Compound subject: A desk and a lamp are in each room.

Compound object: I lost my wallet, my keys, and my watch.

Compound sentence: I don't want to express an opinion, for I don't know much about the subject and I don't want to speak irresponsibly.

condition   A subordinate clause that begins with *if* or *unless.*

Unless all hostility ceases immediately, we will have to take very strong action.

conjunction   A word used to join other words or ideas.

a) *Coordinating* conjunctions join equal or parallel ideas: and, or, nor, but. See Chapter 11.

b) *Correlative* conjunctions are conjunctions used in pairs: *both . . . and, not only . . . but also, neither . . . nor, either . . . or, not . . . but.* See Chapter 11, Section J.

c) *Subordinating* conjunctions join ideas that are not equal or parallel: *when, since, because, after, if, while, as soon as, although, whenever,* and so forth.

d) *Conjunctive adverbs* are transition words like *therefore, nevertheless, however, in fact, still, yet, on the other hand, furthermore, hence, indeed,* and so on. When these words introduce a complete sentence, they should be followed by a comma.

dangling modifier   See Chapter 10.

direct object   A noun, noun clause, or pronoun that receives the action of a verb. It answers the question *whom?* or *what?*

I just read *Barchester Towers.*

What did I just read? *Barchester Towers.*

We hope that they will arrive soon.

What do we hope? That they will arrive soon.

No one knew what had happened.

What did no one know? What had happened.

We shall visit David and Laurie this summer.

Whom shall we visit? David and Laurie.

expletive The words *there* and *it* when they anticipate the real subject of the sentence.

There are several people still unseated.

The real subject is *several people:* Several people are still unseated.

It is useless to argue.

The real subject is *to argue:* To argue is useless.

finite verb A complete verb; a verb that with its subject can stand alone as a complete thought; the verb with its auxiliaries—as opposed to a verbal or a verb form, which are incomplete verbs.

Finite verb: (I) should have gone

Verb form: gone

Verbal: going

gerund A verb form used as a noun.

Subject: *Being mugged* was a frightening experience.

Direct object: We enjoy *sailing.*

I resent your *having lied* to me.

Object of a preposition: I was not responsible for *scratching* the car.

A gerund together with its modifiers is a *gerund phrase:*

Hearing Horowitz perform was an experience I shall never forget.

I was not responsible for *scratching the car.*

imperative A verb form that expresses a command: Get out! Don't be frightened!

impersonal An expression introduced by *it* or *they* for which there is no antecedent.

It is raining.

In the paper *they* say that . . .

It seems to me that . . .

The pronoun *one* is also considered an impersonal pronoun.

One ought to mind one's business.

independent clause   See *clause.*

indirect object   A noun or pronoun that completes the action of verbs of *giving, telling,* or *showing.* The preposition *to* or *for* is always understood.

Tell me [= to me] the story.
Offer him [= to him] the seat.

indirect question   A noun clause used often as the direct object of a verb and introduced by an interrogative word such as *who, what, where, why, when.*

I wondered *where she was.*
We asked *what the commotion was.*
No one knew *who had pulled the alarm.*

indirect statement   A noun clause used often as the direct object of a verb of the senses — for example, *think, believe, know, say, hear,* etc. The word *that* is always stated or implied.

I heard *(that) Margaret went to California.*

Did you know *that Danielle grew up in Spain?*

infinitive   *To* plus a verb form.

I am sorry *to have missed* your performance.

To be drawn and *quartered* must be one of the worst possible tortures.

I helped *(to) clean* the office.

An infinitive together with its modifiers is an *infinitive phrase:*

I am sorry *to have missed your performance.*

To have rescued so frail a creature was an act of great kindness.

I helped *(to) clean the office.*

interjection   A word or group of words that expresses emotion. The interjection is usually followed by an exclamation point or a comma.

Confound it!
Damn!
Aha, now I know.

intransitive verb   A verb that does not take a direct object — for example, *cough.* Most verbs can be either transitive or intransitive depending upon how they are used in the sentence:

INTRANSITIVE: I fled from the police.

TRANSITIVE: I fled the police.

irregular verb   A verb whose past tense is not formed by adding *-d* or *-ed* to the present: catch – caught; see – saw; hold – held.

mood The attitude of a verb toward what it is expressing.

a) The *indicative mood* expresses a fact, statement, or question:

I was going.

Are you going?

b) The *imperative mood* indicates a command:

Go!

Don't get hurt!

c) The *subjunctive mood* expresses something that is not a fact—usually a wish, condition, possibility, or impossibility:

I might go.

You should have gone.

If you were to go, . . .

nominative The name of the case that indicates the subject of a sentence or a noun in the predicate position.

Subject/nominative: The *lawyer* will see you now.

Predicate/nominative: Mr. Rhinelander is a *lawyer*.

noun A word that names a thing, place, person, or idea.

A thing: box, camera, table, war

A place: Louisiana, Mars, Europe

A person: Louise, Mr. Gansa, King Philip

An idea: love, justice, hatred, courage

noun clause See *clause*.

number Whether a word is singular or plural. Nouns, pronouns, and verbs have number.

	Singular	*Plural*
Noun	camera	cameras
	James	Jameses
Pronoun	I	we
	she	they
Verb	am	are
	was	were
	goes	go

numerals A word indicating a number.

A *cardinal* number is one like *one, two, three, four*.

An *ordinal* number is one like *first, second, third, fourth*.

object See *direct object, indirect object, preposition*.

ordinal numerals See *numerals*.

participle   A verb form used as an adjective.

	Active voice	*Passive voice*
Present tense	(while) sending	(while) being sent
Past tense	(having) sent	(having been) sent
Future tense	going to send	going to be sent
	about to send	about to be sent

We heard him *snoring.*

Having walked for several miles, we were exhausted.

The senator squirmed *while being attacked.*

Having been attacked, the senator responded bitterly.

A participle with its modifiers is a *participial phrase.*

While hearing the shouts, we wondered what was happening.

We saw them *defacing the buildings.*

Sometimes a participial phrase is independent of the rest of the sentence. Such a phrase is called an *absolute phrase.*

The arsonist having been captured, the people were relieved.

The storm over, we decided to take a walk.

The second example is elliptical: *the storm over* is equivalent to *the storm being over.*

parts of speech   The different functions that words have as they make up a sentence. There are eight different parts of speech: nouns, verbs, pronouns, adjectives, adverbs, prepositions, conjunctions, and interjections.

passive voice   See discussion of *voice,* Chapter 11.

phrase   A group of words that do not have a subject together with a complete verb. See *prepositional* phrase, *participial* phrase, *appositive* phrase, *infinitive* phrase, *gerund* phrase.

predicate   The predicate indicates what is said of the subject. The predicate includes the verb of the sentence together with its complement(s). (See Section 2 C.)

predicate adjective   An adjective used to complete the meaning of the verb *be* and its affiliates: *become, seem, look, appear, feel, smell, taste, grow, be chosen, be made:*

She looks *sad.*

The material feels *smooth.*

Alex became *angry.*

predicate noun (nominative)   A noun used to complete the meaning of the verb *be* and its affiliates: *become, seem, look, appear, feel, smell, taste, grow, be chosen, be made, be elected, be named.* The noun is a qualification of the subject.

James was elected a class *officer.*

He appears to be the *leader.*

Alex has become an *oil magnate.*

preposition   A word used to express a relationship. It always introduces a noun or a pronoun, and that noun or pronoun is called the *object of the preposition.* The preposition together with its object is called a *prepositional phrase.*

to the city   by Liszt   with an arrow
over the hill   inside the tunnel   after the accident

There is nothing wrong with ending a sentence with a preposition, as long as that sentence does not sound awkward.

Whom have they come for?

A prepositional phrase is not set off by commas:

The assembly met in September with no intention of accepting the proposals submitted by the chairman.

A prepositional phrase that begins a sentence, however, is sometimes set off with a comma to avoid a possible misreading. Thus the sentence:

Because of her, good will and cooperation was widespread.

prevents the reader from the possible misreading:

Because of her good will and cooperation . . .

principal parts of verbs   The basic forms of a verb used to build all the other forms of that verb. There are three principal parts:

The present:	*see*	*go*	*believe*	*help*
The past:	*saw*	*went*	*believed*	*helped*
The past participle:	*seen*	*gone*	*believed*	*helped*

pronoun   See Chapter 4.

restrictive clause   See *clause.*

sentence   A group of words that has a subject and a complete verb form; a sentence always expresses a complete thought. If the sentence is incomplete—that is, if it does not express a complete thought—it is called a *sentence fragment.* (See Chapter 2.)

FRAGMENT: To visit the Philippines.

COMPLETE: I hope to visit the Philippines.

FRAGMENT: Since no one showed up.

COMPLETE: Since no one showed up, the meeting was postponed.

The meeting was postponed since no one showed up.

FRAGMENT: Which is the process by which a piece of skin is transplanted from one part of the body to another.

COMPLETE: Grafting, which is the process by which a piece of skin is transplanted from one part of the body to another, is a most important technique in modern surgery.

subject The noun or pronoun that governs the verb. It answers the question *who?* or *what?*

Timothy and Christopher are fine athletes.

Who are fine athletes? *Timothy and Christopher.* Therefore, *Timothy and Christopher* is the subject of *are.*

Reading detective stories consumed much of his time.

What consumed much of his time? *Reading detective stories.* Therefore, *reading detective stories* is the complete subject of *consumed.*

Do you know why she is so angry?

Does *who* know? *You.* Therefore, *you* is the subject of *know.* *Who* is so angry? *She.* Therefore, *she* is the subject of the verb *is.*

To have performed so well at such a young age indicates enormous talent.

What indicates enormous talent? *To have performed.* Therefore, this infinitive is the simple subject and the whole phrase *to have performed so well at such a young age* is the complete subject of the verb *indicates.*

subordinate clause See *clause.*

subordinate conjunction See *conjunction.*

tense See the discussion of tense in Chapter 11.

verb A word denoting action or state of being. See Chapter 11.

verbal See the discussion of verbals in Chapter 11.

voice See the discussion of voice in Chapter 11.

Bibliography

Readers wishing to pursue in more detail any of the topics covered in this book will find the following works useful.

Grammar and Composition

Beardsley, Monroe C. *Practical Logic*. Englewood Cliffs, N.J.: Prentice-Hall, 1950. See especially Chapter 1.

———. *Thinking Straight*. Englewood Cliffs, N.J.: Prentice-Hall, 1975. See especially Chapter 1.

Brooks, Cleanth, and Robert Penn Warren. *Modern Rhetoric*. New York: Harcourt Brace Jovanovich, 1972.

Butler, Eugenia, et al. *Correct Writing*. Lexington, Mass.: D. C. Heath, 1976.

Jespersen, Otto. *Essentials of English Grammar*. University, Ala.: University of Alabama Press, 1964.

Perrin, Porter G., and George H. Smith. *Handbook of Current English*. New York: Bantam Books, 1966.

Reference Handbook of Grammar and Usage. Prepared by the editorial board of Scott, Foresman and Co., Glenview, Ill., 1972.

Roberts, Paul. *Modern Grammar*. New York: Harcourt Brace Jovanovich, 1968.

Strunk, William, Jr., and E. B. White. *The Elements of Style*. New York: Macmillan, 1972.

Preparation of a Research Paper

Barton, Mary N., and Marion V. Bell. *Reference Books: A Brief Guide for Students and Other Users of the Library*. Baltimore, Md.: Enoch Pratt Free Library, 1970.

Lester, James D. *Writing Reseach Papers: A Complete Guide.* Glenview, Ill.: Scott, Foresman and Co., 1976.

Manual of Style. Prepared by the University of Chicago Press, Chicago, 1969.

MLA Style Sheet. New York: Modern Language Association of America, 1970.

Seeber, Edward D. *Style Manual for Students.* Bloomington, Ind.: University of Indiana Press, 1964.

Theriault, Albert A., Jr. *Guide to Writing Term Papers.* New York: Amsco School Publications, 1971.

Turabian, Kate L. *Manual for the Writers of Term Papers, Theses, and Dissertations.* Chicago: University of Chicago Press, 1973.

————. *Student's Guide for Writing College Papers.* Chicago: University of Chicago Press, 1977.

Diction and Usage

Follett, Wilson. *Modern American Usage.* New York: Warner Paperback Library, 1974.

Fowler, Henry W. *Dictionary of Modern English Usage.* New York: Oxford University Press, 1965.

————, and F. G. Fowler. *The King's English.* New York: Oxford University Press, 1974.

Literature and Literary Terms

Abrams, P. D. *A Glossary of Literary Terms.* New York: Holt, Rinehart, and Winston, 1971.

Beckson, Karl, and Arthur Ganz. *A Reader's Guide to Literary Terms.* New York: The Noonday Press, 1960.

Brooks, Cleanth, et al. *An Approach to Literature.* New York: Appleton-Century-Crofts, 1964.

Holman, C. Hugh. *A Handbook to Literature.* New York: The Odyssey Press, 1972.

Index

Note 1: References in bold type denote a section within a chapter; references in arabic type denote a particular page. Hence, **32T**: 171 indicates section T in Chapter 32, page 171.

Note 2: For a brief definition of terms applying to verbs, consult the table on pages 58–59.

Note 3: For principal parts of irregular verbs, consult the listing of irregular principal parts on pages 70–71.

INDEX

INDEX

INDEX

Elision, 231
Ellipsis, in literature, 232
Ellipsis marks, **25A–25C:**
    149; **33B–33E:**
    177–78
Else, in comparisons, 213
Emend/Amend, 205
Eminent/Imminent, 213
End punctuation, **16A:** 115
End-rhyme, 232
End-stopped, 232
English sonnet, 245
Enjambment, 232
Epic, 232
Epigram, 233
Epitaph, 233
Epithet, 233
Equally, **12S:** 78; 213
Erratic/Sporadic, 213
-es, plurals in, **32K:** 168
Essential clauses, **4K:** 29;
    17E–17F: 123–24;
    17E: 123; 255
et al., **30B:** 158; 184–85
    (footnote 7); **35A:** 190
etc., **18F:** 131; **30B:** 158;
    213
Euphemism, 233
Euphony, 233
Even, **10A:** 54
Ever since, **12G:** 74
Everybody, **3I:** 20; 213
Everyone, **3I:** 20; 213
ex-, **26B:** 150
Exaggeration, 233
Exalt/Exult, 213
Except/Accept, 203
Exclamation point, **19G:**
    134–35; **21B–21G:**
    141–42
Expect/Suspect, 214
Expletives, 258
Exposition, 233
Extended metaphor, 234
Extremely, abuse of, **1C:** 6
Eye rhyme, 234

-f and *-fe,* plurals of, **32R:**
    170
Fable, 234
False rhyme, 234
Fantastic, abuse of, **1B:** 5
Far, comparison of, **9B:** 48
Farther/Further, **9B:** 48;
    214
Faulty coordination,
    13K–13L: 89–91;
    101–102
Faulty parallelism,
    13A–13I: 80–86
Faulty subordination, 102

Feel, **8A–8B:** 44; 214
Feminine ending, 234
Feminine rhyme, 234
Fewer/Less, 214
Figurative language, 234
Figures. *See* Numbers
Figure of sound, 234
Figure of speech, 234
Finite verb, 258
Flashback, 234
Flat character, 227
Flaunt/Flout, 214
Flounder/Founder, 214
Foil, 228
Foot, in poetry, 234–35
Footnotes, 180–88
For, **16G:** 117–18; **16J:**
    118–19
For example, **16H:** 118
For . . . sake, 221
Forbid, **12S:** 78
Foreign words, **27D:** 152;
    32T: 171
Foreshadowing, 235
For instance, **16H:** 118
Formal English, 3
Former/Latter, 214
Founder/Flounder, 214
Fractions, **3J:** 20–21; **26C:**
    150; **29A:** 156
Fragments, **2E:** 15–17;
    16F: 116–17
Free verse, 235
From/Than, **12K:** 174–75
Fulsome, 215
Fun, abuse of, **1G:** 7–8
Further/Farther, **9B:** 48;
    214
Furthermore, **16H:** 118
Fused sentence. *See* Run-
    on sentence
Future/Future perfect
    tense, **11F:** 62–63

Genitive case. *See*
    Possessive case
Geographical names, **18E:**
    130; **31A–31B:** 160–61
Gerund:
    after *Can't help,* **12F:** 73
    defined, 63; 258
    possessive before, **11I:**
    64; 215
Good:
    abuse of, **1B:** 5; **8G:** 46
    comparison of, **9B:** 48
Good/Well, 215
Gothic novel, 235
Grow, as linking verb,
    8C–8D: 44–45
Guttural consonants, 235

270